영문법 판매 1위, 중학영문법 3800제의 초등시리즈

초등영문법 3800제

LEVEL 5

기본1단계

발행 초판 16쇄(2024년 1월 25일)
책임편집 서은숙 **편집** 성은혜 **원고집필** 정다혜, 권은정, 김주현, 정은주, 김유미, 홍주희 **연습문제집필** 조윤경, 권은정, 김송이, 김주희
워크북집필 윤정한, 정다혜, 김주희, 김송이 **원고검토** 유예슬, 최희찬, 박문정, 백경빈, 김미경, 김규은, 양원석, 고민정 **영문감수** Kathryn O'Handley
감수 최주영(대치 위자듀학원 강사) **교정** 황희진, 정다혜, 김주희, 이은영, 하은옥, 홍성경, 오정훈, 심가원, 이은혜, 신영은, 김송이, 하새롬
베타테스트 신재진, 이옥현, 유윤정, 정요한, 신소미, 장신혜, 변선영, 정은주
녹음 와이알 미디어 **녹음대본정리** 신소미, 김소정, 김건탁, 김윤아, 최안나 **녹음검수** 이상미, 신소미, 김소정, 김주희, 윤수경, 이옥현, 이유진, 최안나
사진검색 신의진, 김윤아, 이은혜, 손주연 **삽화** 박현주 **표지디자인** 김연실 **인디자인편집** 정은영, 박정민, 박경아, 김미라, 고연화
제작 이주영 **발행처** ㈜마더텅 **발행인** 문숙영 **주소** 서울시 금천구 가마산로 96, 708호

* 교재 및 기타 문의사항은 **이메일(mothert1004@toptutor.co.kr)**로 보내주시면 감사하겠습니다.
* 이 책에는 네이버에서 제공한 **나눔글꼴**이 적용되어 있습니다.
* 교재 구입 시 온/오프라인 서점에 교재가 없는 경우에는 고객센터 전화 1661-1064(07:00~22:00)로 문의해 주시기 바랍니다.

마더텅 교재를 풀면서 궁금한 점이 생기셨나요?
교재 관련 내용 문의나 오류신고 사항이 있으면 아래 문의처로 보내주세요! 문의하신 내용에 대해 성심성의껏 답변해 드리겠습니다. 또한 교재의 내용 오류 또는 오·탈자, 그 외 수정이 필요한 사항에 대해 가장 먼저 신고해 주신 분께는 감사의 마음을 담아 CU 모바일 편의점 상품권 1천 원권을 보내드립니다!
*기한: 2024년 12월 31일 *오류신고 이벤트는 당사 사정에 따라 조기 종료될 수 있습니다. *홈페이지에 게시된 정오표 기준으로 최초 신고된 오류에 한하여 상품권을 보내드립니다.

카카오톡 mothertongue 이메일 mothert1004@toptutor.co.kr 문자 010-6640-1064(문자수신전용)
홈페이지 www.toptutor.co.kr 교재Q&A게시판 고객센터 전화 1661-1064(07:00~22:00)

초등영문법 3800제 기본1단계

이렇게 공부하세요.

LEVEL 5

STEP 1

문법 개념을 익힌 후 확인테스트를 풀어보면서 제대로 이해했는지 확인해요.

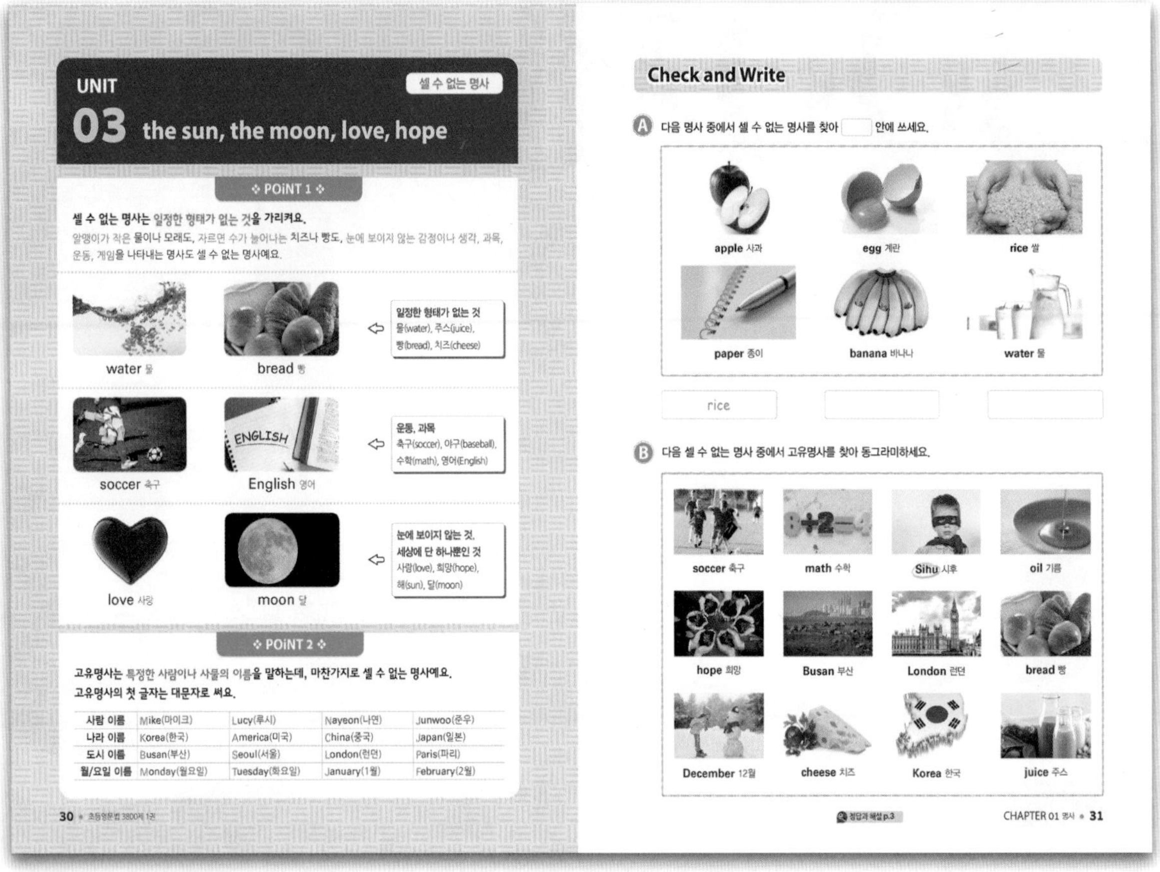
UNIT 03 the sun, the moon, love, hope

셀 수 없는 명사

POiNT 1

셀 수 없는 명사는 일정한 형태가 없는 것을 가리켜요.

알맹이가 작은 물이나 모래도, 자르면 수가 늘어나는 치즈나 빵도, 눈에 보이지 않는 감정이나 생각, 과목, 운동, 게임을 나타내는 명사도 셀 수 없는 명사예요.

water 물 / bread 빵 — 일정한 형태가 없는 것: 물(water), 주스(juice), 빵(bread), 치즈(cheese)

soccer 축구 / English 영어 — 운동, 과목: 축구(soccer), 야구(baseball), 수학(math), 영어(English)

love 사랑 / moon 달 — 눈에 보이지 않는 것, 세상에 단 하나뿐인 것: 사랑(love), 희망(hope), 해(sun), 달(moon)

POiNT 2

고유명사는 특정한 사람이나 사물의 이름을 말하는데, 마찬가지로 셀 수 없는 명사예요. 고유명사의 첫 글자는 대문자로 써요.

사람 이름	Mike(마이크)	Lucy(루시)	Nayeon(나연)	Junwoo(준우)
나라 이름	Korea(한국)	America(미국)	China(중국)	Japan(일본)
도시 이름	Busan(부산)	Seoul(서울)	London(런던)	Paris(파리)
월/요일 이름	Monday(월요일)	Tuesday(화요일)	January(1월)	February(2월)

30 • 초등영문법 3800제 1권

Check and Write

A 다음 명사 중에서 셀 수 없는 명사를 찾아 안에 쓰세요.

apple 사과 / egg 계란 / rice 쌀 / paper 종이 / banana 바나나 / water 물

rice

B 다음 셀 수 없는 명사 중에서 고유명사를 찾아 동그라미하세요.

soccer 축구 / math 수학 / Sihu 시후 / oil 기름 / hope 희망 / Busan 부산 / London 런던 / bread 빵 / December 12월 / cheese 치즈 / Korea 한국 / juice 주스

정답과 해설 p.3

CHAPTER 01 명사 • 31

STEP 2

Practice 1, 2, 3

Practice 1, 2, 3로 구성된 연습문제를 풀면서 앞에서 배운 문법이 적용된 풍부한 예문을 접할 수 있어요. 연습 문제들을 풀다보면, 서술형 문제도 더 이상 어렵지 않아요!

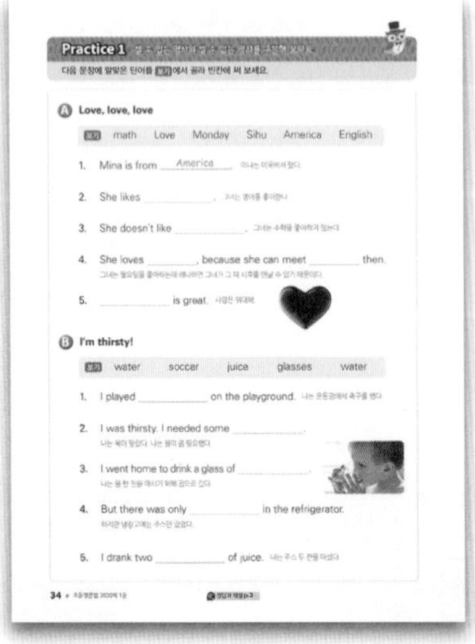
Practice 1

A Love, love, love

math Love Monday Sihu America English

1. Mina is from America.
2. She likes
3. She doesn't like
4. She loves , because she can meet then.
5. is great.

B I'm thirsty!

water soccer juice glasses water

1. I played on the playground.
2. I was thirsty. I needed some
3. I went home to drink a glass of
4. But there was only in the refrigerator.
5. I drank two of juice.

34

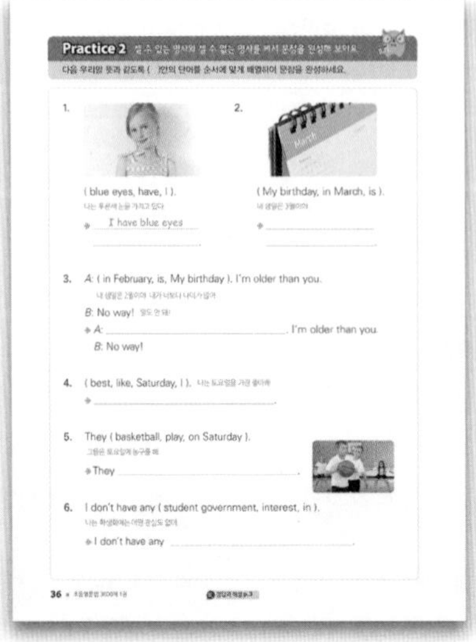
Practice 2

1. (blue eyes, have, I). → I have blue eyes
2. (My birthday, in March, is).
3. A: (in February, is, My birthday). I'm older than you. B: No way! → A: I'm older than you. B: No way!
4. (best, like, Saturday, I).
5. They (basketball, play, on Saturday). → They
6. I don't have any (student government, interest, in). → I don't have any

36

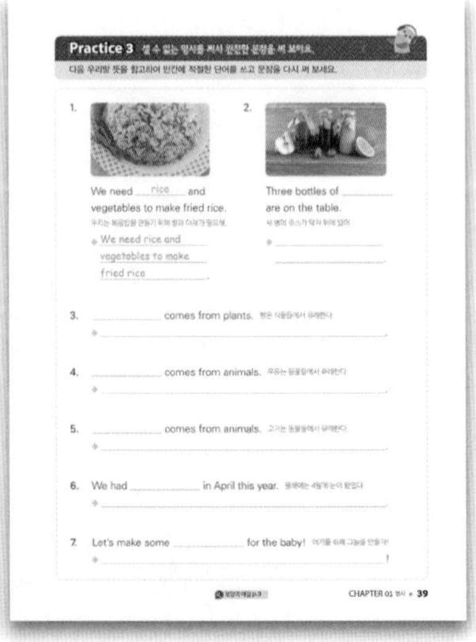
Practice 3

1. We need rice and vegetables to make fried rice. → We need rice and vegetables to make fried rice
2. Three bottles of are on the table.
3. comes from plants.
4. comes from animals.
5. comes from animals.
6. We had in April this year.
7. Let's make some for the baby!

CHAPTER 01 명사 • 39

STEP 3

Let's Practice More!

문법 내용을 제대로 이해했는지 확인할 수 있도록 SET 01–08까지 다양한 유형의 연습문제를 실었어요. 문제를 하나하나 풀다보면 해당 UNIT의 핵심 개념을 제대로 익히게 될 거에요.

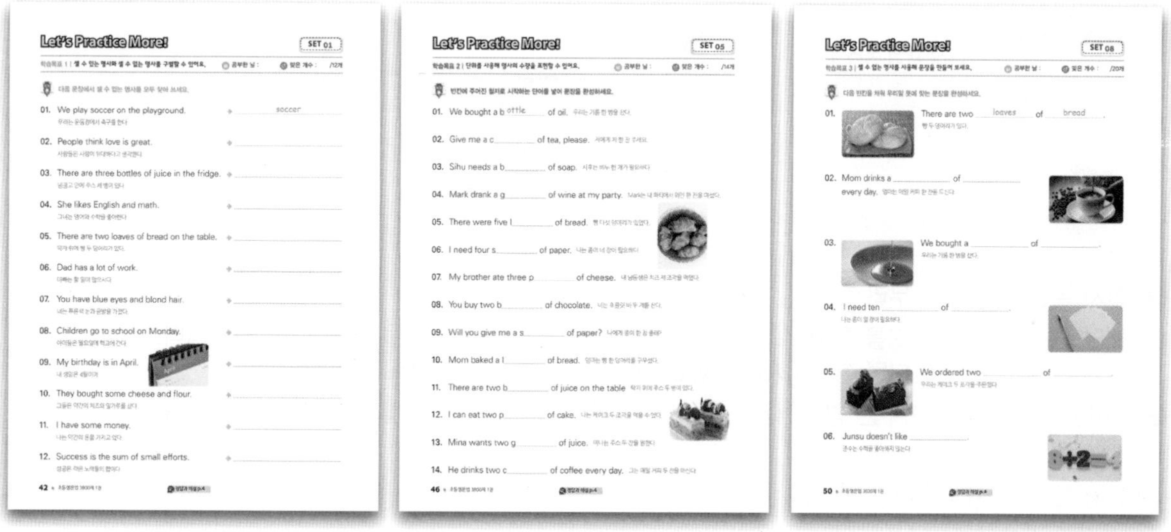

STEP 4

마무리 실전테스트

최종 마무리 테스트로서 권당 2회분의 실전테스트를 실었어요. 총 30문제의 진단평가 및 교내평가 유형의 실전문제로 앞에서 배운 내용을 복습하고 취약한 부분을 파악해 봐요.

워크북 구성 및 활용법 워크북은 아래와 같은 방법으로 활용하세요.

1. 단어쓰기 연습

Chapter 01 부가의문문 Unit 01 부가의문문(1) Unit 02 부가의문문(2)

단어 쓰기 연습 1

MP3 5권 단어 01

들려주는 단어를 잘 듣고, 세 번씩 써 보세요.

01 fat — fat
02 sick — sick
03 lovely — lovely

Chapter 01

MP3 5권 단어 01

들려주는 단어를 잘 듣고, 세 번씩 써 보세요.

14 name — name
15 fight — fight
16 each other — each other
17 wear — wear

❶ 먼저 본문 학습을 마무리 합니다.

❷ 해당 페이지의 QR코드를 통해 스마트 기기로 빠르고 편리하게 음원을 재생할 수 있습니다.
전체 음원 파일은 마더텅 홈페이지(www.toptutor.co.kr)에서 다운로드 가능합니다.

❸ 원어민 선생님이 읽어주는 영단어를 잘 듣고 안내선 안에 영어 단어 철자를 세 번씩 쓰세요.

2. 받아쓰기 시험 (Dictation Test)

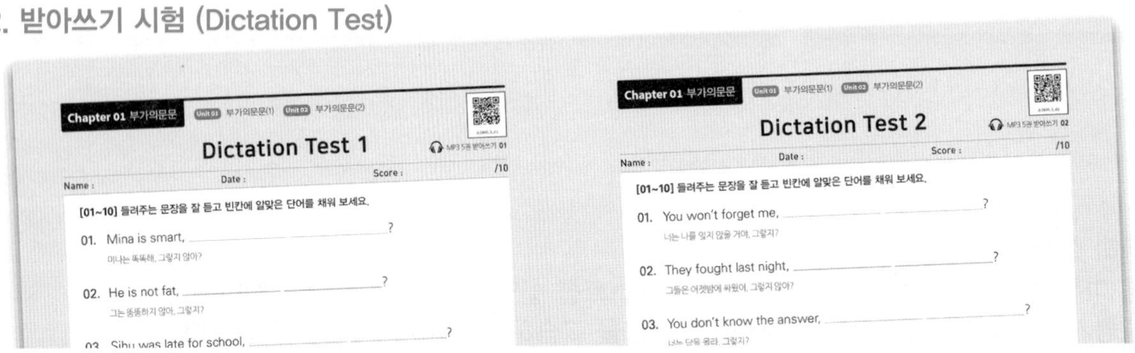
Chapter 01 부가의문문 Unit 01 부가의문문(1) Unit 02 부가의문문(2)

Dictation Test 1

MP3 5권 받아쓰기 01

Name : Date : Score : /10

[01~10] 들려주는 문장을 잘 듣고 빈칸에 알맞은 단어를 채워 보세요.

01. Mina is smart, ______?
미나는 똑똑해, 그렇지 않아?

02. He is not fat, ______?
그는 뚱뚱하지 않아, 그렇지?

03. Sihu was late for school, ______?

Chapter 01 부가의문문 Unit 01 부가의문문(1) Unit 02 부가의문문(2)

Dictation Test 2

MP3 5권 받아쓰기 02

Name : Date : Score : /10

[01~10] 들려주는 문장을 잘 듣고 빈칸에 알맞은 단어를 채워 보세요.

01. You won't forget me, ______?
너는 나를 잊지 않을 거야, 그렇지?

02. They fought last night, ______?
그들은 어젯밤에 싸웠어, 그렇지 않아?

03. You don't know the answer, ______?

❶ 먼저 본문 학습을 마무리 합니다.

❷ 해당 페이지의 QR코드를 통해 스마트 기기로 빠르고 편리하게 음원을 재생할 수 있습니다.
전체 음원 파일은 마더텅 홈페이지(www.toptutor.co.kr)에서 다운로드 가능합니다.

❸ 원어민 선생님이 읽어주는 문장을 잘 듣고, 빈칸을 채우세요.

❹ 받아쓰기 정답은 워크북 뒷부분에 있습니다.

3. 단어테스트

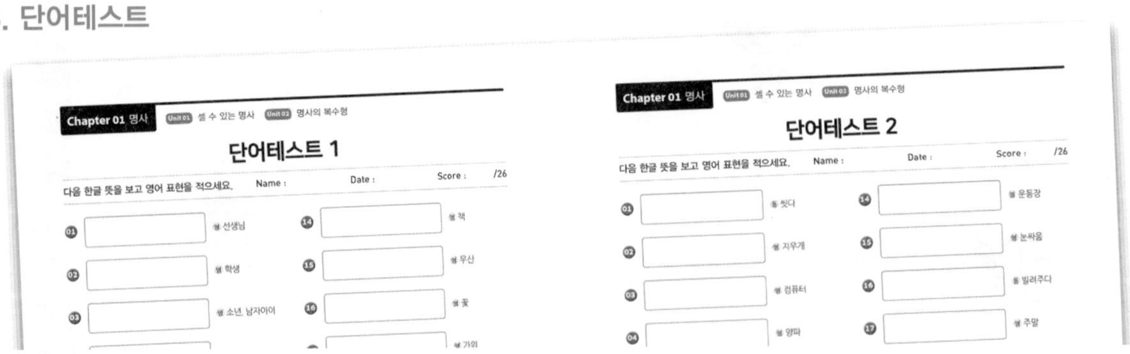
Chapter 01 명사 Unit 01 셀 수 있는 명사 Unit 02 명사의 복수형

단어테스트 1

다음 한글 뜻을 보고 영어 표현을 적으세요. Name : Date : Score : /26

01 명 선생님 14 명 책
02 명 학생 15 명 우산
03 명 소년, 남자아이 16 명 꽃

Chapter 01 명사 Unit 01 셀 수 있는 명사 Unit 02 명사의 복수형

단어테스트 2

다음 한글 뜻을 보고 영어 표현을 적으세요. Name : Date : Score : /26

01 동 씻다 14 명 운동장
02 명 지우개 15 명 눈싸움
03 명 컴퓨터 16 동 빌려주다
04 명 양파 17 명 주말

❶ 단어쓰기 연습을 하며, 단어들을 암기합니다.

❷ 단어테스트의 한글 뜻을 보고 암기한 영단어를 써 보세요.

❸ 학원에서 평가용으로 활용할 수 있고, 스스로 확인하는 용도로 활용할 수도 있습니다.

❹ 단어테스트 정답은 워크북 뒷부분에 있습니다.

4. 워크북 정답

Dictation Test와 단어테스트의 정답을 한 눈에 알아보기 쉬운 형태의 정답지로 제공합니다.

영문법 판매 1위, 중학영문법 3800제의 초등시리즈

초등영문법 3800제

LEVEL 5

기본1단계 CONTENTS

Chapter 01 부가의문문

이 챕터에서는 상대방에게 확인이나 동의를 구할 때
문장 뒤에 덧붙이는 '부가의문문'에 대해 배워 보아요.

☆ 학습 방향 및 배울 내용 미리보기 ☆

☐ **Unit 01 :** Sihu is tall, **isn't he?**
부가의문문 (1)
부가의문문을 만들 때 지켜야 할 규칙을 알아보아요.

▼

☐ **Unit 02 :** You ate some pizza, **didn't you?**
부가의문문 (2)
문장에서 be동사, 일반동사, 조동사가 쓰일 때, 부가의문문이 각각의 경우에 어떻게 쓰이는지 알아보아요.

단어 미리보기

이 챕터에 나올 단어들 중 이미 알고 있는 단어가 있나요?
맞는 뜻을 골라 체크해 봐요.

날짜 : 이름 : 알고 있는 단어의 수 : /24개

No.	아는 단어	단어	품사	알맞은 뜻에 체크 표시해 봐요.			
1	☑	fat	형용사	뚱뚱한	☑	마른	☐
2	☐	sick	형용사	건강한	☐	아픈	☐
3	☐	childish	형용사	어른스러운	☐	어린아이 같은	☐
4	☐	smart	형용사	똑똑한	☐	멍청한	☐
5	☐	clothes	명사	신발	☐	옷	☐
6	☐	still	부사	여전히	☐	일찍	☐
7	☐	break	동사	연결하다	☐	부러뜨리다	☐
8	☐	week	명사	주	☐	주말	☐
9	☐	headache	명사	치통	☐	두통	☐
10	☐	fish	동사	낚시하다	☐	헤엄치다	☐
11	☐	perfect	형용사	서투른	☐	완벽한	☐
12	☐	answer	명사	답	☐	오류	☐
13	☐	forget	동사	잊다	☐	기억하다	☐
14	☐	clean	형용사	깨끗한	☐	더러운	☐
15	☐	change	명사	한결같음	☐	변화	☐
16	☐	alone	형용사	혼자인	☐	함께인	☐
17	☐	fear	동사	두려워하다	☐	즐거워하다	☐
18	☐	Chinese	명사	중국어	☐	일본어	☐
19	☐	cook	명사	전자레인지	☐	요리사	☐
20	☐	boring	형용사	지루한	☐	흥미로운	☐
21	☐	close	동사	열다	☐	닫다	☐
22	☐	swim	동사	흔들다	☐	수영하다	☐
23	☐	disappointed	형용사	실망한	☐	기쁜	☐
24	☐	will	조동사	~할 수 있다	☐	~할 것이다	☐

UNIT 01 Sihu is tall, isn't he?

부가의문문 (1)

❖ POiNT 1 ❖

부가의문문이란?

'그렇지 않아?' '그렇지?' '안 그래?' 와 같이 상대방에게 확인이나 동의를 구하고 싶을 때 문장 뒤에 덧붙이는 의문문을 말해요.

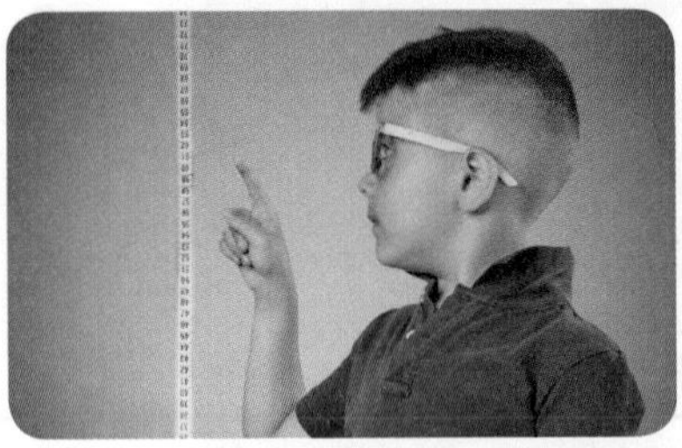

Sihu is tall, isn't he? 시후는 키가 커, 그렇지 않아?

Sihu isn't fat, is he? 시후는 뚱뚱하지 않아, 그렇지?

❖ POiNT 2 ❖

부가의문문 만들기 (be동사)

부가의문문을 만들기 위해서는 네 가지 규칙을 지켜야 해요.

1 앞의 문장이 긍정이면 부정의 부가의문문을, 앞의 문장이 부정이면 긍정의 부가의문문을 써요.

Sihu is tall, isn't he? / Sihu isn't fat, is he?
긍정 부정 부정 긍정

2 부가의문문의 주어는 인칭대명사(you, he, she, it, they, we)로 바꿔줘요.

Sihu is tall, isn't he?

3 부가의문문의 동사가 부정형이면 축약형으로 써요.

Sihu is tall, isn't he?

4 부가의문문의 동사의 시제는 앞의 문장과 같은 시제를 사용해야 해요!

Sihu is tall, isn't he?

Sihu was sick, wasn't he?

Check and Write

A 다음 빈칸에 들어갈 부가의문문을 쓰세요.

1. Kelly is so lovely, [isn't she?]
   Kelly는 매우 사랑스러워, 그렇지 않니?

2. The movie was fun, [ ]
   그 영화는 재밌었어, 그렇지 않았니?

3. You are not a liar, [ ]
   너는 거짓말쟁이가 아니야, 그렇지?

B 다음 중 알맞은 것에 동그라미하세요.

1. My brother is childish, (isn't / is not) he?
   내 남동생은 어린애 같아, 그렇지 않니?

2. Her hair is not short, (isn't it / is it)?
   그녀의 머리는 짧지 않아, 그렇지?

3. These are yummy, aren't (they / it)?
   이것들은 맛있어, 그렇지 않니?

정답과 해설 p.2

부가의문문 (2)

UNIT 02 You ate some pizza, didn't you?

❖ POiNT ❖

부가의문문의 동사별 사용법

부가의문문은 앞 문장의 주어와 동사의 시제 · 종류에 따라 조금씩 달라져요!

be동사

Sihu is tall, isn't he?
시후는 키가 커, 그렇지 않니?

일반동사

Mina likes pizza, doesn't she?
미나는 피자를 좋아해, 그렇지 않니?

They don't like pizza, do they?
그들은 피자를 안 좋아해, 그렇지?

You ate some pizza, didn't you?
너는 피자를 먹었어, 그렇지 않니?

조동사

He can go hiking, can't he?
그는 하이킹을 갈 수 있어, 그렇지 않니?

She should go hiking, shouldn't she?
그녀는 하이킹을 가야 해, 그렇지 않니?

You will go hiking, won't you?
너는 하이킹을 갈 거야, 그렇지 않니?

Check and Write

다음 빈칸에 들어갈 부가의문문을 쓰고, 전체 문장을 다시 쓰세요.

1. Mina doesn't like Sihu, [does she]?
미나는 시후를 좋아하지 않아, 그렇지?
➔ Mina doesn't like Sihu, does she ?

2. You got a haircut, [ ]?
너는 머리를 잘랐어, 그렇지 않니?
➔ ____________________?

3. He can play soccer, [ ]?
그는 축구를 할 수 있어, 그렇지 않니?
➔ ____________________?

4. They will help you, [ ]?
그들은 당신을 도와줄 거예요, 그렇지 않나요?
➔ ____________________?

5. You are from China, [ ]?
너는 중국에서 왔어, 그렇지 않니?
➔ ____________________?

6. The baby is cute, [ ]?
그 아기는 귀여워, 그렇지 않니?
➔ ____________________?

정답과 해설 p.2

Practice 1 문제를 풀면서 부가의문문을 익혀 보아요.

다음 문장에 알맞은 단어를 보기에서 골라 빈칸에 써 보세요. (중복 사용 가능)

A Mina's family

보기 isn't aren't wasn't

1. Mina is smart, ___isn't___ she? 미나는 똑똑해, 그렇지 않아?

2. Mina's little brother is so cute, ______________ he?
미나의 남동생은 정말 귀여워, 그렇지 않아?

3. Mina and her brother are tall, ______________ they?
미나와 그녀의 남동생은 키가 커, 그렇지 않아?

4. Her mother was a teacher, ______________ she?
그녀의 엄마는 선생님이셨어, 그렇지 않아?

5. Her parents are both 40 years old,
______________ they?
그녀의 부모님은 두 분 다 40살이셔, 그렇지 않아?

B I'm angry!

보기 didn't don't isn't doesn't

1. Nayeon has a twin sister named Nari,
______________ she?
나연이는 나리라는 쌍둥이 여동생이 있어, 그렇지 않아?

2. They fought last night, ______________ they?
그들은 어젯밤에 싸웠어, 그렇지 않아?

3. They always get along with each other, ______________ they?
그들은 항상 서로 잘 지내잖아, 그렇지 않아? (*get along with: ~와 잘 지내다)

정답과 해설 p.2

4. Nari wore Nayeon's favorite clothes, ______________ she?
나리는 나연이가 가장 좋아하는 옷을 입었어, 그렇지 않아?

5. Nayeon is still angry, ______________ she?
나연이는 여전히 화가 나있어, 그렇지 않아?

C Piano contest

보기 won't can't will

1. You can play the piano, ______________ you?
너는 피아노를 칠 수 있어, 그렇지 않아?

2. You will play the piano at a concert, ______________ you?
너는 연주회에서 피아노를 연주할거야, 그렇지 않아?

3. You won't go to the piano academy, ______________ you?
너는 피아노 학원에 다니지 않을 거야, 그렇지?

4. You will practice hard, ______________ you?
너는 열심히 연습할 거야, 그렇지 않아?

5. You can do well, ______________ you?
너는 잘 할 수 있어, 그렇지 않아?

D Why was he late?

보기 didn't wasn't did

1. Sihu was late for school, ______________ he? 시후는 학교에 늦었어, 그렇지 않아?

2. He didn't wake up late, ______________ he? 그는 늦게 일어나지 않았어, 그렇지?

3. He didn't play soccer yesterday, ______________ he?
그는 어제 축구를 안 했어, 그렇지?

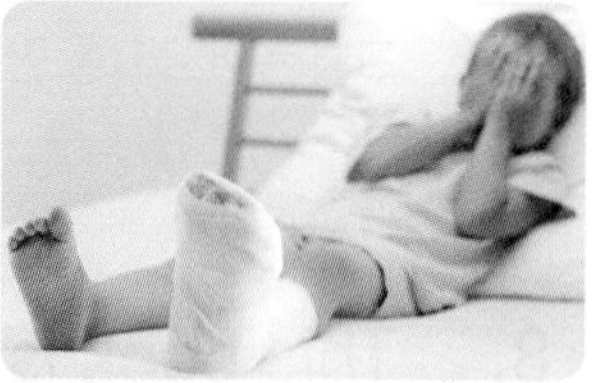

4. He broke his leg, ______________ he?
그는 다리가 부러졌어, 그렇지 않아?

5. He fell down the stairs, ______________ he?
그는 계단에서 넘어졌어, 그렇지 않아?

정답과 해설 p.2

Practice 2 부가의문문을 써서 확인, 동의를 구하는 문장을 써 보아요.

다음 (   ) 안의 표현 중 알맞은 것에 동그라미 하세요.

1. 

She is crying, (is / isn't) she?

그녀는 울고 있어, 그렇지 않아?

2. 

They will go fishing, (will / won't) they?

그들은 낚시하러 갈 예정이야, 그렇지 않니?

3. You (went / didn't go) skiing last week, didn't you?

너는 지난주에 스키 타러 갔어, 그렇지 않아?

4. She (looks / doesn't look) sick, doesn't she?

그녀는 아파 보여, 그렇지 않아?

5. She doesn't have a headache, (does / doesn't) she?

그녀는 두통이 있진 않잖아, 그렇지?

6. She (breaks up / broke up) with her boyfriend, didn't she?

그녀는 남자친구와 헤어졌어, 그렇지 않아?

7. She (doesn't meet / didn't meet) him yesterday, did she?

그녀는 어제 그를 만나지 않았어, 그렇지?

8. This book is boring, isn't (he / it)?

이 책은 지루해, 그렇지 않니?

정답과 해설 p.2

9.

He (can / could) bake apple pies, can't he?
그는 사과파이를 구울 수 있어, 그렇지 않아?

10.

She can play the violin, (can't / couldn't) she?
그녀는 바이올린을 연주할 수 있어, 그렇지 않아?

11. He likes soccer, (doesn't / didn't) he?
그는 축구를 좋아해, 그렇지 않아?

12. He is not fat, (is / are) he?
그는 뚱뚱하지 않아, 그렇지?

13.

He likes chicken salad, (don't / doesn't) he?
그는 치킨 샐러드를 좋아해, 그렇지 않니?

14.

She can't write in English, can (you / she)?
그녀는 영어로 글을 쓸 수 없어, 그렇지?

15. He runs fast, (don't / doesn't) he?
그는 빨리 달려, 그렇지 않아?

16. Mr. Lee likes pizza, doesn't (he / she)?
이 선생님은 피자를 좋아하셔, 그렇지 않니?

정답과 해설 p.2

17.

They are twins, aren't (we / they)?

그들은 쌍둥이구나, 그렇지 않아?

18.

He wants to be a cook, doesn't (he / she)?

그는 요리사가 되고 싶어 해, 그렇지 않아?

19.

Clara can't swim well, can (she / you)?

Clara는 수영을 잘하지 못해, 그렇지?

20.

You didn't go to bed early, did (he / you)?

너는 일찍 잠자리에 들지 않았어, 그렇지?

Cultural Tips
재미로 익히는 문화상식

세계의 여름방학

우리나라 초등학생들은 7월 중순부터 8월 중순까지 약 4주간의 여름방학을 보내요.
그런데 미국의 초등학생들은 5월 말부터 8월 말까지 약 12주 동안 여름방학을 보낸답니다.
게다가 아주 더운 지역인 이집트에서는 6월부터 9월 중순까지 길게는 무려 15주 동안 여름 방학을 보낸다고 해요!
이웃나라 일본은 여름방학이 7월 중순에서 8월 말까지로 우리나라와 비슷해요!

정답과 해설 p.2

Practice 3 부가의문문을 써서 문장을 완성해 보아요.

우리말 해석을 참고하여 빈칸에 알맞은 부가의문문을 쓰세요.

1. 

He likes watching movies, ___doesn't he___?
그는 영화 보는 것을 좋아해, 그렇지 않아?

2. 

He can play baseball, ____________?
그는 야구를 할 수 있어, 그렇지 않아?

3. His sister doesn't like reading books, ____________?
그의 여동생은 책 읽는 것을 좋아하지 않아, 그렇지?

4. His father was a baseball player, ____________?
그의 아빠는 야구선수였어, 그렇지 않아?

5. He and his friends always go to the park, ____________?
그와 그의 친구들은 항상 공원에 가, 그렇지 않아?

6. Nayeon went to China last year, ____________?
나연이는 작년에 중국에 갔어, 그렇지 않아?

7. Her parents work in China, ____________?
그녀의 부모님은 중국에서 일하셔, 그렇지 않아?

8. She speaks Chinese, ____________?
그녀는 중국어를 (말)해, 그렇지 않아?

정답과 해설 p.2

9. She can't read Chinese, ____________________?

그녀는 중국어를 읽을 수 없어, 그렇지?

10. 

Chinese isn't easy,

____________________?

중국어는 쉽지 않아, 그렇지?

11. 

The bank closes at 4 p.m.,

____________________?

은행은 오후 4시에 문을 닫아, 그렇지 않아?

12. Sihu went to the bank at 5 p.m., ____________________?

시후는 오후 5시에 은행에 갔어, 그렇지 않아?

13. He was disappointed, ____________________?

그는 실망했어, 그렇지 않아?

14. 

The doll is very big,

____________________?

그 인형은 매우 커, 그렇지 않니?

15. 

It was a perfect day for a picnic, ____________________?

소풍 가기에 완벽한 날이었어, 안 그래?

16. People always fear change, ____________________?

사람들은 항상 변화를 두려워해요, 그렇지 않나요?

정답과 해설 p.2

17. 

We are not alone,

____________________?

우리는 혼자가 아니야, 그렇지?

18. 

The room is clean,

____________________?

그 방은 깨끗해, 안 그러니?

19. 

You will not forget me,

____________________?

너는 나를 잊지 않을 거야, 그렇지?

20. 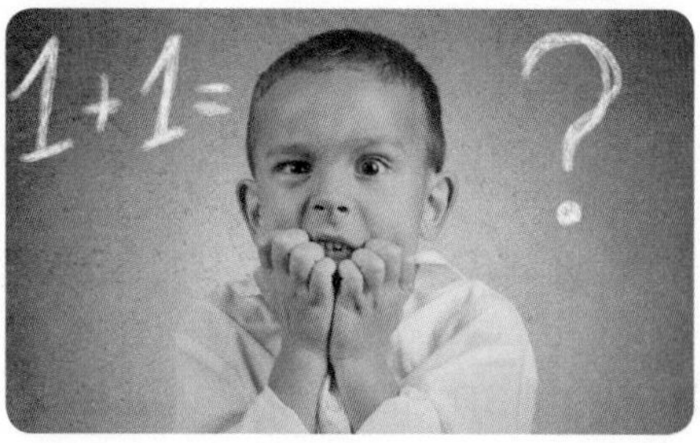

You don't know the answer,

____________________?

너는 답을 몰라, 그렇지?

Cultural Tips
재미로 익히는 문화상식

새 학기가 시작되는 날도 나라마다 달라?

미국은 보통 8월 말이나 9월 초에 새로운 학년이 시작돼요. 그리고 1월 중순에 2학기 수업에 들어가 5월 말에 학기가 마무리 된답니다.

일본은 4월 1일에 새 학년이 시작되고, 3월에 한 학년이 끝나요.

오스트레일리아(호주)는 1월 말 또는 2월 초에 새 학기가 시작돼요.

한국은 보통 3월에 새 학년이 시작되는데, 새 학기가 시작되는 날이 나라마다 다르다니 신기하지 않나요?

정답과 해설 p.2

Let's Practice More!

SET 01

학습목표 1 | be동사를 활용한 부가의문문을 알아보아요. 공부한 날 : 맞은 개수 : /12개

다음 문장을 읽고 밑줄 친 부분이 맞으면 ○표, 틀리면 ×표를 하세요.

01. Mina and I are in the same class, are we? → ×
미나와 나는 같은 반이야, 그렇지 않니?

02. His father was a baseball player, wasn't him? 그의 아빠는 야구선수였어, 그렇지 않니? → ______

03. Your brother is tall and kind, isn't he? → ______
너의 오빠는 키가 크고 친절해, 그렇지 않니?

04. You and Brian are on vacation, aren't you? → ______
너와 Brian은 휴가 중이야, 그렇지 않니?

05. Mike was disappointed, wasn't Mike? → ______
Mike는 실망했어, 그렇지 않니?

06. You aren't tired, aren't you? → ______
너는 피곤하지 않아, 그렇지?

07. The doll wasn't big, was it? 그 인형은 크지 않았어, 그렇지? → ______

08. Today is Monday, isn't today? 오늘은 월요일이야, 그렇지 않니? → ______

09. Chinese isn't easy, isn't it? 중국어는 쉽지 않아, 그렇지? → ______

10. They are twins, weren't they? → ______
그들은 쌍둥이야, 그렇지 않니?

11. This book is boring, isn't it? → ______
이 책은 지루해, 그렇지 않니?

12. We are not alone, are we? 우리는 혼자가 아니야, 그렇지? → ______

정답과 해설 p.2

Let's Practice More!

SET 02

학습목표 1 | be동사를 활용한 부가의문문을 알아보아요.   공부한 날 :   맞은 개수 :   /14개

다음 (   ) 안에서 알맞은 것을 고르세요.

01. You are on vacation, (are / aren't) you? 너는 휴가 중이야, 그렇지 않니?

02. Sihu was late for school, wasn't (he / him)?
시후는 학교에 늦었어, 그렇지 않니?

03. Mina is smart, (isn't / wasn't) she?
미나는 똑똑해, 그렇지 않니?

04. He isn't fat, (is / isn't) he? 그는 뚱뚱하지 않아, 그렇지?

05. Today is Sunday, isn't (it / today)? 오늘은 일요일이야, 그렇지 않니?

06. Sihu and I are both 13 years old, (are / aren't) we? 시후와 나는 둘 다 13살이야, 그렇지 않니?

07. Mina's little brother is so cute, (isn't / wasn't) he?
미나의 남동생은 정말 귀여워, 그렇지 않아?

08. Her mother was a teacher, (isn't / wasn't) she? 그녀의 엄마는 선생님이셨어, 그렇지 않아?

09. This game isn't boring, is (it / this game)? 이 게임은 지루하지 않아, 그렇지?

10. The elephant was big, (was / wasn't) it?
그 코끼리는 컸어, 그렇지 않니?

11. They are tired, aren't (they / them)?
그들은 피곤해, 그렇지 않니?

12. Mike was happy, wasn't (he / Mike)?
Mike는 행복했어, 그렇지 않니?

13. Jane was a police officer, (isn't / wasn't) she?
Jane은 경찰관이었어, 그렇지 않니?

14. Jisu and Mina weren't in the same class, (were / weren't) they?
지수와 미나는 같은 반이 아니었어, 그렇지?

정답과 해설 p.2

Let's Practice More!

SET 03

학습목표 2 | 동사에 따라 달라지는 부가의문문을 연습해 보아요. 공부한 날 : 맞은 개수 : /14개

다음 ( ) 안에서 알맞은 표현을 고르세요.

01. Sihu went to the bank at 5 p.m., (don't / didn't) he?
시후는 오후 5시에 은행에 갔어, 그렇지 않니?

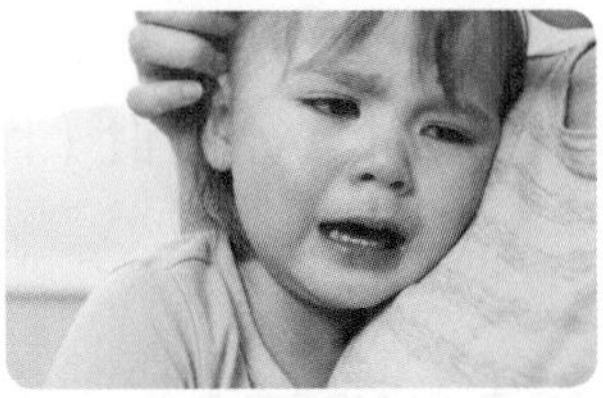

02. She is crying, (isn't / wasn't) she?
그녀는 울고 있어, 그렇지 않니?

03. She can't read Chinese, (can / can't) she? 그녀는 중국어를 읽을 수 없어, 그렇지?

04. Nayeon has a twin sister named Nari, (doesn't / don't) she?
나연이는 나리라는 쌍둥이 여동생이 있어, 그렇지 않니?

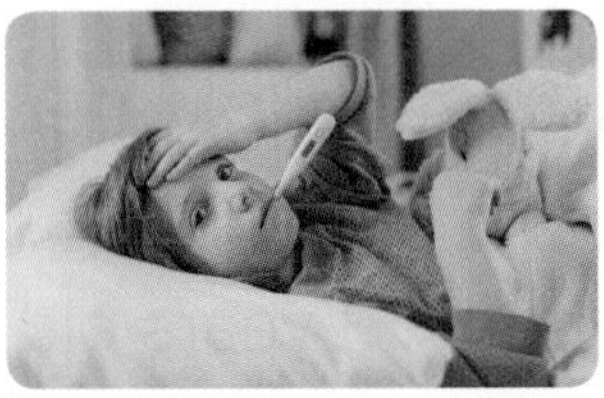

05. She looks sick, (doesn't / didn't) she?
그녀는 아파 보여, 그렇지 않니?

06. The room is clean, (is / isn't) it?
그 방은 깨끗해, 그렇지 않니?

07. Her parents work in China, (don't / didn't) they?
그녀의 부모님은 중국에서 일하셔, 그렇지 않니?

08. People always fear change, (aren't / don't) they?
사람들은 항상 변화를 두려워 해, 그렇지 않니?

09. You don't know the answer, (do / don't) you? 너는 답을 몰라, 그렇지?

10. Nayeon is still angry, (isn't / aren't) she?
나연이는 여전히 화가 나있어, 그렇지 않니?

11. Mina and her brother are tall, (isn't / aren't) they?
미나와 그녀의 남동생은 키가 커, 그렇지 않니?

12. He likes chicken salad, (doesn't / didn't) he? 그는 치킨 샐러드를 좋아해, 그렇지 않니?

13. It was a perfect day for a picnic, (isn't / wasn't) it?
소풍 가기에 완벽한 날이었어, 그렇지 않니?

14. She doesn't have a headache, (does / do) she? 그녀는 두통이 있지 않아, 그렇지?

정답과 해설 p.2

Let's Practice More!

SET 04

학습목표 2 | 동사에 따라 달라지는 부가의문문을 연습해 보아요. 공부한 날 : 맞은 개수 : /14개

다음 빈칸에 알맞은 부가의문문을 쓰세요.

01. You can play the flute, ___can't you___?
너는 플루트를 연주할 수 있어, 그렇지 않니?

02. He didn't play soccer yesterday, ______________?
그는 어제 축구를 안 했어, 그렇지?

03. She broke up with her boyfriend, ______________?
그녀는 남자친구와 헤어졌어, 그렇지 않니?

04. He runs fast, ______________? 그는 빨리 달려, 그렇지 않니?

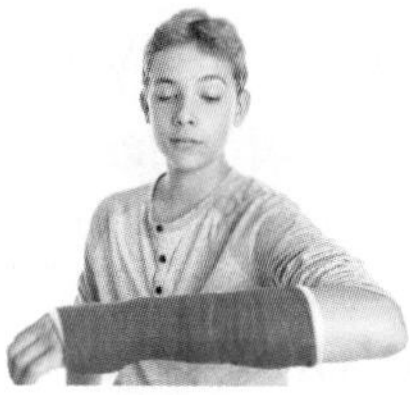

05. He broke his arm, ______________?
그는 팔이 부러졌어, 그렇지 않니?

06. She didn't meet him yesterday, ______________?
그녀는 어제 그를 만나지 않았어, 그렇지?

07. He can bake apple pies, ______________? 그는 사과파이를 구울 수 있어, 그렇지 않니?

08. You will play the piano at a concert, ______________?
너는 연주회에서 피아노를 연주할거야, 그렇지 않니?

09. You can do well, ______________? 너는 잘 할 수 있어, 그렇지 않니?

10. Mr. Lee likes pizza, ______________? 이 선생님은 피자를 좋아하셔, 그렇지 않니?

11. He wants to be a cook, ______________? 그는 요리사가 되고 싶어 해, 그렇지 않니?

12. Clara can't swim well, ______________?
Clara는 수영을 잘하지 못해, 그렇지?

13. You don't know the answer, ______________?
너는 답을 몰라, 그렇지?

14. He fell down the stairs, ______________? 그는 계단에서 넘어졌어, 그렇지 않니?

정답과 해설 p.2

Let's Practice More!

SET 05

학습목표 2 | 동사에 따라 달라지는 부가의문문을 연습해 보아요.　공부한 날 :　맞은 개수 :　/12개

다음 (　) 안에서 알맞은 표현을 고르세요.

01. He was disappointed, (wasn't / didn't) he?
그는 실망했어, 그렇지 않니?

02. She can't write in English, (does / can) she?
그녀는 영어로 글을 쓸 수 없어, 그렇지?

03. The bank closes at 4 p.m., (doesn't / won't) it?
그 은행은 오후 4시에 문을 닫아, 그렇지 않니?

04. The doll is very big, (isn't / doesn't) it?
그 인형은 매우 커, 그렇지 않니?

05. Her parents work in China, (aren't / don't) they?
그녀의 부모님은 중국에서 일하셔, 그렇지 않니?

06. Clara can't swim well, (does / can) she? Clara는 수영을 잘하지 못해, 그렇지?

07. Sihu went to the bank at 5 p.m., (weren't / didn't) he?
시후는 오후 5시에 은행에 갔어, 그렇지 않니?

08. We are not alone, (are / don't) we? 우리는 혼자가 아니야, 그렇지?

09. Nayeon went to China last year, (wasn't / didn't) she?
나연이는 작년에 중국에 갔어, 그렇지 않니?

10. They will go fishing, (don't / won't) they? 그들은 낚시하러 갈 예정이야, 그렇지 않니?

11. You will practice hard, (don't / won't) you?
너는 열심히 연습할 거야, 그렇지 않니?

12. It was a perfect day for a picnic, (wasn't / didn't) it?
소풍 가기에 완벽한 날이었어, 그렇지 않니?

정답과 해설 p.2

Let's Practice More!

SET 06

학습목표 2 | 동사에 따라 달라지는 부가의문문을 연습해 보아요. 공부한 날 : 맞은 개수 : /14개

다음 빈칸에 알맞은 부가의문문을 쓰세요.

01. You won't go to the piano academy, ______will you______?
너는 피아노 학원에 다니지 않을 거야, 그렇지?

02. He didn't wake up late, ____________? 그는 늦게 일어나지 않았어, 그렇지?

03. You will practice hard, ____________? 너는 열심히 연습할 거야, 그렇지 않니?

04. You can do well, ____________? 너는 잘 할 수 있어, 그렇지 않니?

05. We are hungry, ____________? 우리는 배고파, 그렇지 않니?

06. Sihu was late for school, ____________?
시후는 학교에 늦었어, 그렇지 않니?

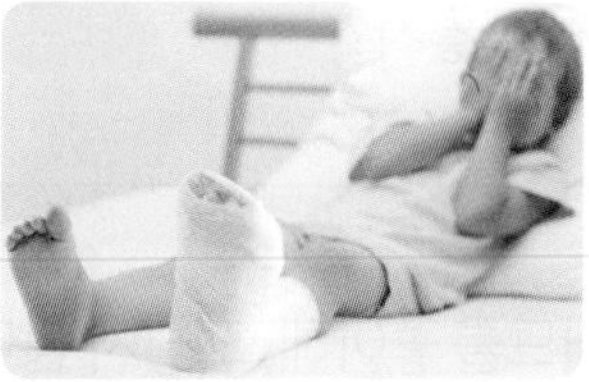

07. He broke his leg, ____________?
그는 다리가 부러졌어, 그렇지 않니?

08. They went skiing last week, ____________?
그들은 지난주에 스키 타러 갔어, 그렇지 않니?

09. She has a headache, ____________?
그녀는 두통이 있어, 그렇지 않니?

10. This book is boring, ____________? 이 책은 지루해, 그렇지 않니?

11. We can play the violin, ____________? 우리는 바이올린을 연주할 수 있어, 그렇지 않니?

12. She looks sick, ____________? 그녀는 아파 보여, 그렇지 않니?

13. They are twins, ____________?
그들은 쌍둥이야, 그렇지 않니?

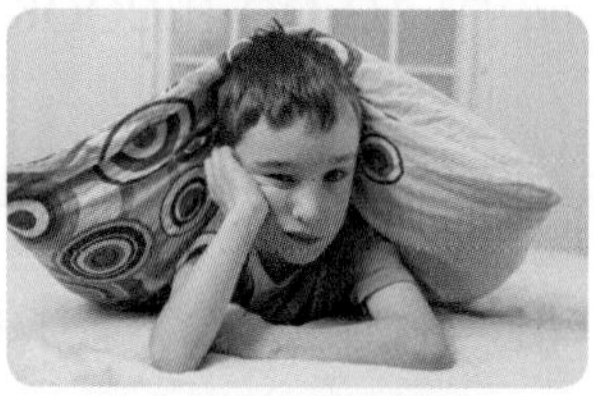

14. You didn't go to bed early, ____________?
너는 일찍 잠자리에 들지 않았어, 그렇지?

정답과 해설 p.2

Let's Practice More!

SET 07

학습목표3 | 알맞은 부가의문문을 써 보아요.　　공부한 날 :　　맞은 개수 :　　/20개

다음 문장이 주어진 우리말 해석과 같은 뜻이 되도록 빈칸을 완성해 보세요.

01. 

그들은 축구를 좋아해, 그렇지 않아?

They like soccer, <u>don't they</u>?

02. 

그 방은 깨끗해, 안 그러니?

The room is clean, ______________?

03. 그녀는 중국어를 읽을 수 없어, 그렇지?

She can't read Chinese, ______________?

04. 그는 뚱뚱하지 않아, 그렇지?

He isn't fat, ______________?

05. 민준이는 치킨 샐러드를 좋아해, 그렇지 않니?

Minjun likes chicken salad, ______________?

06. 너의 여동생은 빨리 달려, 그렇지 않아?

Your sister runs fast, ______________?

07. 너는 피아노를 칠 수 있어, 그렇지 않아?

You can play the piano, ______________?

08. 너의 아빠는 야구를 하실 수 있어, 그렇지 않아?

Your father can play baseball, ______________?

09. 너는 요리사가 되고 싶어 해, 그렇지 않아?

You want to be a cook, ______________?

10. 그 여자애는 피아노 학원에 다니지 않을 거야, 그렇지?

The girl won't go to the piano academy, ______________?

정답과 해설 p.2

11.

이 선생님은 피자를 좋아하셔,
그렇지 않니?

Mr. Lee likes pizza,
_______________?

12.

너는 연주회에서 피아노를 연주할거야,
그렇지 않아?

You will play the piano at
a concert, _______________?

13. 나의 이모는 영화 보는 것을 좋아해, 그렇지 않아?

My aunt likes watching movies, _______________?

14. 중국어는 쉽지 않아, 그렇지?

Chinese isn't easy, _______________?

15. 우리는 사과파이를 구울 수 있어, 그렇지 않아?

We can bake apple pies, _______________?

16. 그의 아빠는 야구선수야, 그렇지 않아?

His father is a baseball player, _______________?

17. 그녀는 울고 있어, 그렇지 않아?

She is crying, _______________?

18. 그 아이들은 영어로 글을 쓸 수 없어, 그렇지?

The children can't write in English, _______________?

19. 그녀의 부모님은 두 분 다 40살이셔, 그렇지 않아?

Her parents are both 40 years old, _______________?

20. 그의 여동생은 책 읽는 것을 좋아하지 않아, 그렇지?

His sister doesn't like reading books, _______________?

정답과 해설 p.2

Let's Practice More!

SET 08

학습목표3 | 알맞은 부가의문문을 써 보아요. 　　공부한 날 : 　　맞은 개수 : 　　/20개

다음 문장이 주어진 우리말 해석과 같은 뜻이 되도록 빈칸을 완성해 보세요.

01. 

그녀는 여전히 화가 나있어, 그렇지 않아?

She is still angry, isn't she ?

02. 

그들은 어젯밤에 싸웠어, 그렇지 않아?

They fought last night, ________________?

03. 그녀의 엄마는 선생님이셔, 그렇지 않아?

Her mother is a teacher, ________________?

04. 사람들은 항상 변화를 두려워해요, 그렇지 않나요?

People always fear change, ________________?

05. 나연이는 나리라는 쌍둥이 여동생이 있어, 그렇지 않아?

Nayeon has a twin sister named Nari, ________________?

06. 시후는 학교에 늦었어, 그렇지 않아?

Sihu was late for school, ________________?

07. 너는 잘 할 수 있어, 그렇지 않아?

You can do well, ________________?

08. 너는 열심히 연습할 거야, 그렇지 않아?

You will practice hard, ________________?

09. 그녀는 바이올린을 연주할 수 있어, 그렇지 않아?

She can play the violin, ________________?

정답과 해설 p.2

10. 미나와 그녀의 남동생은 키가 커, 그렇지 않아?
Mina and her brother are tall, ________________?

11. 

그들은 항상 서로 잘 지내잖아, 그렇지 않아?
They always get along with each other, ________________?

12. 

그녀는 남자친구와 헤어졌어, 그렇지 않아?
She broke up with her boyfriend, ________________?

13. 그들은 낚시하러 갈 예정이야, 그렇지 않아?
They will go fishing, ________________?

14. 미나의 남동생은 정말 귀여워, 그렇지 않아?
Mina's little brother is so cute, ________________?

15. 이 책은 지루해, 그렇지 않아?
This book is boring, ________________?

16. 그는 계단에서 넘어졌어, 그렇지 않아?
He fell down the stairs, ________________?

17. 나리는 나연이가 가장 좋아하는 옷을 입었어, 그렇지 않아?
Nari wore Nayeon's favorite clothes, ________________?

18. 미나는 똑똑해, 그렇지 않아?
Mina is smart, ________________?

19. Clara는 수영을 잘하지 못해, 그렇지?
Clara can't swim well, ________________?

20. 그녀는 어제 그를 만나지 않았어, 그렇지?
She didn't meet him yesterday, ________________?

정답과 해설 p.2

Chapter 02 수량형용사

이 챕터에서는 사물의 수량이 얼마나 되는지를 나타내는 형용사인
'수량형용사'에 대해 배워 보아요.

☆ 학습 방향 및 배울 내용 미리보기 ☆

▢ Unit 01 : I have **many** books.

many와 much

many와 much를 써서 셀 수 있는 명사와 셀 수 없는 명사의 많음을 표현할 수 있어요.

▢ Unit 02 : I can see **a lot of** horses.

a lot of와 lots of

a lot of와 lots of를 쓰면 셀 수 있는 명사와 셀 수 없는 명사의 구분 없이 많음을 표현할 수 있어요.

▢ Unit 03 : I eat **a few** doughnuts.

a few와 a little

a few와 a little을 써서 셀 수 있는 명사와 셀 수 없는 명사의 적음을 표현할 수 있어요.

▢ Unit 04 : I can see **few** flowers.

few와 little

few와 little을 써서 셀 수 있는 명사와 셀 수 없는 명사의 거의 없음을 표현할 수 있어요. 이 때 문장은 부정문처럼 해석돼요.

▢ Unit 05 : I want to drink **some** water.

some과 any

대략적인 수나 양을 표현하는 some과 any가 각각 어떤 문장에 쓰이는지 알아보아요.

▢ Unit 06 : **All** students go to school every day.

all과 every

'모두', '전체'의 의미를 가지는 all과 every가 각각 어떤 명사와 같이 쓰이는지 알아보아요.

단어 미리보기

이 챕터에 나올 단어들 중 이미 알고 있는 단어가 있나요?
맞는 뜻을 골라 체크해 봐요.

날짜 : 　　이름 : 　　알고 있는 단어의 수 : /24개

No.	아는 단어	단어	품사	알맞은 뜻에 체크 표시해 봐요.			
1	☑	begin	동사	시작하다	☑	끝마치다	☐
2	☐	plant	명사	동물	☐	식물	☐
3	☐	ant	명사	개미	☐	지렁이	☐
4	☐	light	형용사	가벼운	☐	무거운	☐
5	☐	work	명사	휴식	☐	일	☐
6	☐	lesson	명사	듣기	☐	교훈	☐
7	☐	mushroom	명사	버섯	☐	거실	☐
8	☐	order	동사	주문하다	☐	오르다	☐
9	☐	here	부사	거기에	☐	여기에	☐
10	☐	onion	명사	양파	☐	마늘	☐
11	☐	silver	형용사	은색의	☐	금색의	☐
12	☐	harmful	형용사	유익한	☐	해로운	☐
13	☐	trouble	명사	문제	☐	여행	☐
14	☐	exercise	명사	예	☐	운동	☐
15	☐	learn	동사	배우다	☐	가르치다	☐
16	☐	empty	형용사	가득한	☐	빈	☐
17	☐	raw	형용사	날 것의	☐	익힌	☐
18	☐	paint	동사	그리다	☐	지우다	☐
19	☐	idea	명사	생각	☐	사랑	☐
20	☐	true	형용사	진짜의	☐	거짓의	☐
21	☐	cloud	명사	풀밭	☐	구름	☐
22	☐	may	조동사	~해야 한다	☐	~일지도 모른다	☐
23	☐	pass	동사	통과하다	☐	떨어지다	☐
24	☐	daughter	명사	아들	☐	딸	☐

UNIT 01 I have many books.

수량형용사란?

수량의 많고 적음을 나타내는 형용사를 '수량형용사'라고 해요.
먼저 '많음'을 나타내는 대표적인 표현에는 many, much가 있어요.

❖ POiNT 1 ❖

many 셀 수 있는 명사의 복수형 앞에 쓰여 '많은, 다수의'의 의미를 나타내요.

긍정문	I have **many** books. 나는 많은 책들을 가지고 있어.
부정문	I don't have **many** shoes. 나는 신발들이 많지 않아.
의문문	Do you have **many** brothers? 너는 형제들이 많아?

many books

many shoes

many brothers

❖ POiNT 2 ❖

much 셀 수 없는 명사 앞에 쓰여 '많은, 다량의'의 의미를 나타내요.
긍정문보다는 부정문, 의문문에 더 자주 쓰여요.

부정문	I don't have **much** time. 나는 시간이 많지 않아.
의문문	Do you have **much** money? 너는 많은 돈을 가지고 있어?

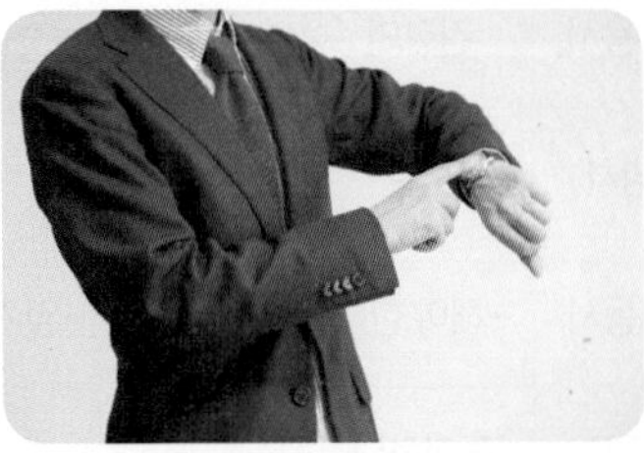
much time

much money

Check and Write

A 다음 빈칸에 many와 much 중 알맞은 단어를 써보세요.

1. 

many cats

2. 

_____ cars

3. 

_____ love

4. 

_____ rain

5. 

_____ boxes

6. 

_____ cheese

B 다음 ( )에서 알맞은 단어에 동그라미하고, 문장을 다시 쓰세요.

1. I bought many (potato / potatoes).

→ I bought many potatoes.

나는 많은 감자를 샀어.

2. I don't have many (clothes / cloth).

→ ______________________________.

나는 옷을 많이 갖고 있지 않아.

3. We had (many / much) rain yesterday.

→ ______________________________.

어제는 많은 비가 내렸어.

정답과 해설 p.3

UNIT 02 I can see a lot of horses.

a lot of와 lots of

셀 수 있는 명사인지 셀 수 없는 명사인지 구분하기 어렵다면, 둘 중 어디에나 쓸 수 있는 a lot of 나 lots of를 쓰면 돼요.

❖ POiNT 1 ❖

a lot of / lots of

a lot of와 lots of는 셀 수 있는 명사의 복수형, 셀 수 없는 명사에 둘 다 쓸 수 있어요.
또한 긍정문, 부정문, 의문문에 모두 쓸 수 있어요.

긍정문	I can see **a lot of[lots of]** horses. 나는 많은 말들을 볼 수 있어.
부정문	I don't need **a lot of[lots of]** carrots. 나는 많은 당근들이 필요하지 않아.
의문문	Did you buy **a lot of[lots of]** bread? 너는 많은 빵을 샀어?

❖ POiNT 2 ❖

a lot of / lots of가 셀 수 있는 명사와 쓰인 경우

a lot of horses
lots of horses

a lot of carrots
lots of carrots

a lot of flowers
lots of flowers

❖ POiNT 3 ❖

a lot of / lots of가 셀 수 없는 명사와 쓰인 경우

a lot of milk
lots of milk

a lot of sand
lots of sand

a lot of bread
lots of bread

Check and Write

A 다음 ( )에서 알맞은 단어에 모두 동그라미하세요.

1.

I eat (many / much / a lot of / lots of) tomatoes.

2.

Instant noodles have (many / much / a lot of / lots of) salt.

B 다음 ( )에서 알맞은 단어에 동그라미하고, 문장을 다시 쓰세요.

1. I get a lot of (flower / flowers).

➔ I get a lot of flowers.

나는 많은 꽃을 받는다.

2. I want to drink (many / a lot of) juice.

➔ ______________________.

나는 주스를 많이 마시고 싶어.

3. We make (lots of / much) mistakes.

➔ ______________________.

우리는 실수를 많이 해.

정답과 해설 p.3

Practice 1 많음을 표현하는 수량형용사를 익혀 보아요.

many, much 중 알맞은 단어를 빈칸에 써 보세요.

A In the kitchen

1. ___many___ dishes 많은 그릇들

2. ________ juice 많은 주스

3. ________ bread 많은 빵

4. ________ bananas 많은 바나나들

5. ________ water 많은 물

B In my room

1. ________ comic books 많은 만화책들

2. ________ trash 많은 쓰레기

3. ________ toys 많은 장난감들

4. ________ sunlight 많은 햇살

5. ________ pillows 많은 베개들

정답과 해설 p.3

C Baking cookies!

1. I will spend __________ time baking cookies.
   나는 쿠키를 굽는 데 많은 시간을 쓸 거야.

2. __________ friends like my cookies.
   많은 친구들이 내 쿠키를 좋아해.

3. I don't need __________ butter. 나는 많은 버터가 필요하진 않아.

4. I bought __________ eggs at the supermarket.
   나는 슈퍼마켓에서 많은 계란들을 샀어.

5. I used too __________ flour. 나는 너무 많은 밀가루를 썼어.

D In Spring

1. __________ schools start a new semester.
   많은 학교들이 새 학기를 시작해.

2. __________ flowers begin to bloom.
   많은 꽃들이 피기 시작해.

3. We can grow __________ plants.
   우리는 많은 식물들을 키울 수 있어.

4. We don't have __________ rain in June. 6월에는 많은 비가 내리지 않아.

5. __________ yellow dust comes from China in spring.
   봄에는 많은 황사 먼지가 중국에서 불어와.

정답과 해설 p.3

Practice 2 명사에 따라 달라지는 수량형용사의 알맞은 쓰임을 익혀 보아요.

다음 (   )에서 알맞은 것에 동그라미 하세요.

1.

She eats (many / much) cheese.

그녀는 많은 치즈를 먹어.

2.

You need (many / much) flour.

너는 많은 밀가루가 필요해.

3. They drank (many / a lot of) beer yesterday.

그들은 어제 많은 맥주를 마셨어.

4. He saved (many / much) money.

그는 많은 돈을 모았어.

5. We buy (many / much) apples.

우리는 많은 사과들을 사.

6. You can find (much / a lot of) ants in the hole.

너는 그 구멍에서 많은 개미들을 발견할 수 있어.

7. She has (much / a lot of) pencils.

그녀는 많은 연필들을 갖고 있어.

정답과 해설 p.3

8.

Ice cream has (many / lots of) sugar.

아이스크림에는 많은 설탕이 들어있어.

9.

My uncle ate (many / a lot of) meat.

나의 삼촌은 많은 고기를 먹었어.

10.

He drinks (many / lots of) milk.

그는 많은 우유를 마셔.

11.

He eats too (many / much) pepper. (*pepper: 후추)

그는 너무 많은 후추를 먹어.

12. He doesn't have (much / a lot of) toys.

그는 많은 장난감들을 갖고 있지 않아.

13.

Do you have (many / much) cousins? (*cousin: 사촌)

너는 사촌들이 많니?

14.

Drink (many / a lot of) water for your health.

당신의 건강을 위해 많은 물을 마시세요.

정답과 해설 p.3

15. She has (many / much) friends.
그녀는 친구들이 많아.

16.

They bought (much / a lot of) balloons for her birthday party.
그들은 그녀의 생일 파티를 위해 많은 풍선들을 샀어.

17.

I could see (much / lots of) people at the stadium.
(*stadium: 경기장)

나는 경기장에서 많은 사람들을 볼 수 있었어.

18.

We don't have (many / much) time.
우리는 시간이 많지 않아.

19.

I take care of (many / much) pets.
나는 많은 애완동물들을 돌봐.

20. She has (much / a lot of) shoes.
그녀는 많은 신발들을 갖고 있어.

정답과 해설 p.3

Practice 3 수량형용사를 써서 문장을 완성해 보아요.

다음 우리말 뜻과 같도록 주어진 표현을 순서에 맞게 배열하여 문장을 완성하세요.
(단, 수량형용사는 명사 앞에 오도록 배열하세요.)

1. (study, many, subjects, I).
나는 많은 과목들을 공부해. (*subject: 과목)

→ I study
many subjects.

2. (much, homework, have, I).
나는 숙제가 많아.

→ ______________________
______________________.

3. (I don't have, time, much) to play with my friends.
나는 나의 친구들과 놀 시간이 많지 않아.

→ ______________________ to play with my friends.

4. (stress, a lot of, I have). 나 스트레스 많이 받아.

→ ______________________.

5. (much, I didn't take, rest). (*rest: 휴식)
나는 많은 휴식을 취하지 못했어.

→ ______________________.

6. (worry about, Many, their health, people). 많은 사람들이 그들의 건강을 걱정해.

→ ______________________.

7. (should not put, You, sugar, a lot of) into the bowl.
너는 그릇에 많은 설탕을 넣지 말아야 해.

→ ______________________
into the bowl.

정답과 해설 p.3

8. (shouldn't drink, coffee, too much, We).
우리는 너무 많은 커피를 마셔서는 안 돼.

➔ ______________________________
______________________________.

9. (salt, much, You, should not eat).
너는 많은 소금을 먹어서는 안 돼.

➔ ______________________________
______________________________.

10. (languages, many, learns, She). 그녀는 많은 언어들을 배워.

➔ ____.

11. (you, spend, Did, time, a lot of) with her?
너는 그녀와 많은 시간을 함께 보냈어?

➔ ____ with her?

12. Yes, (asked, I, questions, many) about her American life.
응, 나는 그녀의 미국 생활에 대해 많은 질문들을 했어.

➔ Yes, ___________________________________ about her American life.

13. (took, photos, We, a lot of).
우리는 많은 사진들을 찍었어.

➔ ______________________________
______________________________.

14. (lots of, He, Coke, drinks).
그는 많은 콜라를 마셔.

➔ ______________________________
______________________________.

정답과 해설 p.3

15. (Mother Teresa, people, helped, a lot of).

테레사 수녀는 많은 사람들을 도왔어.

➔ ______________________________

______________________________.

16. (a lot of, She, heard, good news).

그녀는 많은 좋은 소식들을 들었어.

➔ ______________________________

______________________________.

17. (make, light work, hands, Many). 많은 손들이 일을 가볍게 만든다. (백지장도 맞들면 낫다.)

➔ ______________________________

______________________________.

18. (a shower, Many, make, drops). (*shower: 소나기, drop: (빗)방울)

많은 빗방울들이 모여 소나기를 만든다. (티끌 모아 태산이다.)

➔ ______________________________.

19. (cooks, Too many, the broth, spoil). (*spoil: 망치다, broth: 수프, cook: 요리사)

너무 많은 요리사들은 수프를 망친다. (사공이 많으면 배가 산으로 간다.)

➔ ______________________________.

20. (has, The world, lessons, many) to teach you.

세상은 당신에게 가르쳐줄 많은 교훈들을 가지고 있어요.

➔ ______________________________ to teach you.

정답과 해설 p.3

Let's Practice More!

SET 01

학습목표 1 | many와 much의 쓰임을 익혀 보아요.　　공부한 날 :　　맞은 개수 :　　/12개

다음 (　)에서 알맞은 것에 ○표 하세요.

01. (many / much) sugar 많은 설탕

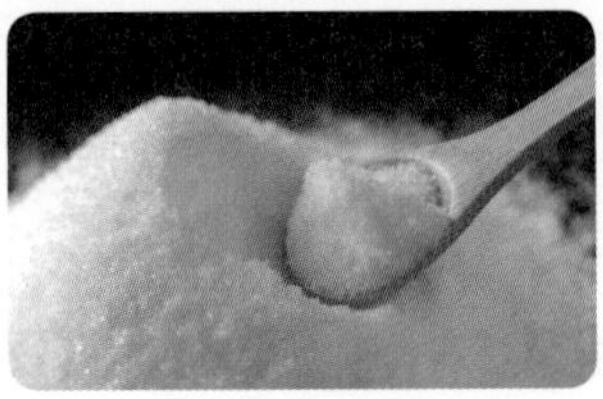

02. (many / much) sunlight 많은 햇살

03. (many / much) dishes 많은 그릇들

04. (many / much) bananas 많은 바나나들

05. (many / much) money 많은 돈

06. (many / much) milk 많은 우유

07. (many / much) apples 많은 사과들

08. (many / much) water 많은 물

09. (many / much) friends 많은 친구들

10. (many / much) cheese 많은 치즈

11. (many / much) homework 많은 숙제

12. (many / much) eggs 많은 계란들

정답과 해설 p.3

Let's Practice More!

SET 02

학습목표 1 | many와 much의 쓰임을 익혀 보아요.　　공부한 날 :　　맞은 개수 : 　/14개

밑줄 친 부분이 맞으면 ○표, 틀리면 바르게 고쳐 쓰세요.

01. I learn much languages. 나는 많은 언어들을 배워. → many

02. He doesn't have many time to play with his friends. → ________
그는 그의 친구들과 놀 시간이 많지 않아.

03. My mom bought many pillows. → ________
나의 엄마는 많은 베개들을 사셨어.

04. You can grow much plants. → ________
너는 많은 식물들을 키울 수 있어.

05. Many schools start a new semester. → ________
많은 학교들이 새 학기를 시작해.

06. She takes care of many pets. → ________
그녀는 많은 애완동물들을 돌봐.

07. My dad should not eat many salt. 나의 아빠는 많은 소금을 드셔서는 안 돼. → ________

08. He studies much subjects. 그는 많은 과목들을 공부해. → ________

09. Does she have much cousins? 그녀는 사촌들이 많니? → ________

10. He needs much flour. 그는 많은 밀가루가 필요해. → ________

11. You eat too many pepper. 너는 너무 많은 후추를 먹어. → ________

12. Much yellow dust comes from China in spring. → ________
봄에는 많은 황사 먼지가 중국에서 불어와.

13. We don't have much rain in June. → ________
6월에는 많은 비가 내리지 않아.

14. You shouldn't drink too many coffee. → ________
너는 너무 많은 커피를 마셔서는 안 돼.

정답과 해설 p.3

Let's Practice More!

SET 03

학습목표 1 | many와 much의 쓰임을 익혀 보아요.   공부한 날 :   맞은 개수 :   /14개

다음 주어진 단어 앞에 many와 much 중 적절한 수량형용사를 써서 빈칸을 완성하세요.

01. cheese → much cheese 많은 치즈

02. oranges → ______________ 많은 오렌지들

03. lessons → ______________ 많은 교훈들

04. languages → ______________ 많은 언어들

05. rest → ______________ 많은 휴식

06. flowers → ______________ 많은 꽃들

07. bread → ______________ 많은 빵

08. time → ______________ 많은 시간

09. people → ______________ 많은 사람들

10. pets → ______________ 많은 애완동물들

11. dishes → ______________ 많은 그릇들

12. questions → ______________ 많은 질문들

13. juice → ______________ 많은 주스

14. hands → ______________ 많은 손들

정답과 해설 p.3

Let's Practice More!

SET 04

학습목표 2 | many, much, a lot of, lots of의 개념을 확실히 다져 보아요. 공부한 날 : 맞은 개수 : /12개

many, much, a lot of, lots of 중 ( )에 들어갈 수 있는 것을 두 개 고르세요.

01. I don't have (many / much / a lot of) money.
나는 많은 돈을 갖고 있지 않아.

02. He drank (many / much / lots of) beer yesterday.
그는 어제 많은 맥주를 마셨어.

03. We can find (many / much / lots of) ants in the hole.
우리는 그 구멍에서 많은 개미들을 발견할 수 있어.

04. His dad ate (many / much / a lot of) meat. 그의 아빠는 많은 고기를 드셨어.

05. They have (many / much / a lot of) pencils. 그들은 많은 연필들을 갖고 있어.

06. You don't have (many / much / lots of) toys. 너는 많은 장난감들을 갖고 있지 않아.

07. Drink (many / much / a lot of) water for your health.
당신의 건강을 위해 많은 물을 마시세요.

08. I bought (many / much / lots of) balloons for her birthday party. 나는 그녀의 생일 파티를 위해 많은 풍선들을 샀어.

09. He took (many / much / lots of) photos.
그는 많은 사진들을 찍었어.

10. My mom has (many / much / a lot of) stress.
나의 엄마는 스트레스를 많이 받아.

11. Did he spend (many / much / a lot of) time with her?
그가 그녀와 함께 많은 시간을 보냈어?

12. She should not put (many / much / a lot of) sugar into the bowl.
그녀는 그릇에 많은 설탕을 넣지 말아야 해.

정답과 해설 p.3

Let's Practice More!

SET 05

학습목표 2 | many, much, a lot of, lots of의 개념을 확실히 다져 보아요. 　공부한 날 : 　맞은 개수 : /14개

밑줄 친 부분이 맞으면 ○표, 틀리면 ×표 하세요.

01. I don't have <u>many</u> time. 나는 많은 시간을 갖고 있지 않아. → ×

02. They buy <u>a lot of</u> apples. →
그들은 많은 사과들을 사.

03. She saved <u>much</u> money. →
그녀는 많은 돈을 모았어.

04. He used too <u>much</u> flour. →
그는 너무 많은 밀가루를 썼어.

05. There is so <u>many</u> trash in my room. →
아주 많은 쓰레기가 내 방에 있어.

06. I bought <u>many</u> eggs at the supermarket. →
나는 슈퍼마켓에서 많은 계란들을 샀어.

07. <u>Much</u> people worry about their health. →
많은 사람들이 그들의 건강을 걱정해.

08. They heard <u>a lot of</u> good news. 그들은 많은 좋은 소식들을 들었어. →

09. He asked <u>lots of</u> questions about my American life. →
그는 나의 미국 생활에 대해 많은 질문들을 했어.

10. The world has <u>much</u> lessons to teach me. →
세상은 나에게 가르쳐줄 많은 교훈들을 가지고 있다.

11. We didn't take <u>many</u> rest. 우리는 많은 휴식을 취하지 못했어. →

12. Too <u>much</u> cooks spoil the broth. →
너무 많은 요리사들은 수프를 망친다. (사공이 많으면 배가 산으로 간다.)

13. <u>Many</u> flowers begin to bloom. →
많은 꽃들이 피기 시작해.

14. We have <u>lots of</u> comic books. →
우리는 많은 만화책들을 갖고 있어.

정답과 해설 p.3

Let's Practice More!

SET 06

학습목표 3 | a lot of, lots of의 쓰임을 익혀 보아요. 공부한 날 : 맞은 개수 : /14개

다음 문장에서 'a lot of', 'lots of'가 셀 수 있는 명사를 꾸며주면 'C'를, 셀 수 없는 명사를 꾸며주면 'UC'를 쓰세요.

01. He drank lots of water. 그는 많은 물을 마셨어. → UC

02. I have a lot of pencils. → ______
나는 많은 연필들을 갖고 있어.

03. She doesn't have a lot of toys. → ______
그녀는 많은 장난감들을 갖고 있지 않아.

04. My brother ate lots of meat. 나의 남동생은 많은 고기를 먹었어. → ______

05. They took lots of photos. 그들은 많은 사진들을 찍었어. → ______

06. The baby drinks a lot of milk. → ______
그 아기는 많은 우유를 마셔.

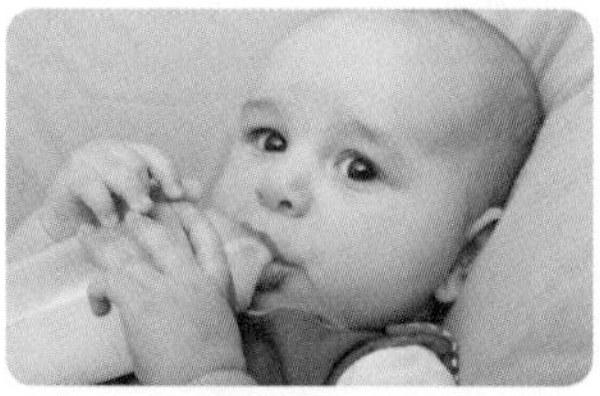

07. Ice cream has lots of sugar. → ______
아이스크림에는 많은 설탕이 들어있어.

08. We could see a lot of people at the stadium. → ______
우리는 경기장에서 많은 사람들을 볼 수 있었어.

09. We bought lots of balloons for his birthday party. → ______
우리는 그의 생일 파티를 위해 많은 풍선들을 샀어.

10. Did you spend a lot of time with your mom? → ______
너는 너의 어머니와 함께 많은 시간을 보냈어?

11. Mother Teresa helped lots of people. → ______
테레사 수녀는 많은 사람들을 도왔어.

12. You drink lots of Coke. 너는 많은 콜라를 마셔. → ______

13. We can find a lot of ants in the hole. → ______
우리는 그 구멍에서 많은 개미들을 발견할 수 있어.

14. My sister has a lot of shoes. 나의 언니는 많은 신발을 갖고 있어. → ______

정답과 해설 p.4

Let's Practice More!

SET 07

학습목표 3 | a lot of, lots of의 쓰임을 익혀 보아요.   공부한 날 :   맞은 개수 :   /20개

다음 밑줄 친 부분 대신 much를 쓸 수 있으면 ○표, 쓸 수 없으면 ×표 하세요.

01. 

He drinks lots of Coke.

그는 많은 콜라를 마셔.

→ ○

02. 

My grandmother takes care of a lot of pets.

나의 할머니는 많은 애완동물들을 돌보셔.

→ ______

03. I have a lot of pencils. 나는 많은 연필들을 갖고있어. → ______

04. There is a lot of trash in my brother's room. → ______

많은 쓰레기가 나의 남동생의 방에 있어.

05. I don't have a lot of energy. → ______

나는 기운이 많지 않아.

06. She will spend lots of time baking cookies. → ______

그녀는 쿠키를 굽는 데 많은 시간을 쓸 거야.

07. They eat lots of bread. 그들은 많은 빵을 먹어. → ______

08. Her mom bought a lot of pillows. 그녀의 엄마는 많은 베개들을 샀어. → ______

09. They don't have lots of time. 그들은 시간이 많지 않아. → ______

정답과 해설 p.4

10. He saved lots of money. 그는 많은 돈을 모았어. → ____________

11. 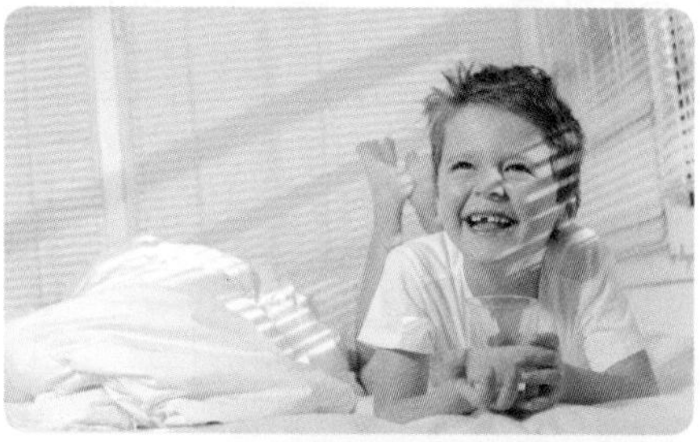

There is a lot of sunlight in my room. 내 방에는 많은 햇살이 들어.

→ ____________

12. 

She has lots of stress. 그녀는 스트레스를 많이 받아.

→ ____________

13. You don't have a lot of time to play with your friends. 너는 너의 친구들과 놀 시간이 많지 않아. → ____________

14. Lots of friends like her cookies. 많은 친구들이 그녀의 쿠키를 좋아해. → ____________

15. You can grow a lot of plants. 너는 많은 식물들을 키울 수 있어. → ____________

16. Her dad drank lots of beer yesterday. 그녀의 아빠는 어제 많은 맥주를 마셨어. → ____________

17. They learn lots of languages. 그들은 많은 언어들을 배워. → ____________

18. He drinks a lot of juice. 그는 많은 주스를 마셔. → ____________

19. Does he have lots of cousins? 그는 사촌들이 많니? → ____________

20. We study a lot of subjects. 우리는 많은 과목들을 공부해. → ____________

정답과 해설 p.4

Let's Practice More!

SET 08

학습목표 4 | 많음을 표현하는 수량형용사를 이용하여 다양한 표현을 만들어 보아요.

공부한 날 :　　　맞은 개수 :　　/20개

( )에서 알맞은 것을 고르세요.

01. 

I want (much / a lot of) fruits.
나는 많은 과일들을 원해요.

02. 

We eat (many / much) bread.
우리는 많은 빵을 먹어.

03. She has (much / a lot of) dishes. 그녀는 많은 그릇들을 갖고 있어.

04. My mom drinks (many / lots of) water.
나의 엄마는 많은 물을 마셔.

05. He doesn't need (many / much) butter. 그는 많은 버터가 필요하진 않아.

06. She has (many / much) homework. 그녀는 숙제가 많아.

07. My mom bought (much / a lot of) eggs at the supermarket.
나의 엄마는 슈퍼마켓에서 많은 계란들을 샀어.

08. Ice cream has (many / lots of) sugar. 아이스크림에는 많은 설탕이 들어있어.

09. My sister didn't take (many / lots of) rest.
나의 언니는 많은 휴식을 취하지 못했어.

10. I have (much / a lot of) shoes. 나는 많은 신발들을 갖고 있어.

정답과 해설 p.4

11. 

(Many / Much) flowers begin to bloom.
많은 꽃들이 피기 시작해.

12. 

He has (much / lots of) friends.
그는 친구들이 많아.

13. (Much / A lot of) people worry about their health.
많은 사람들이 그들의 건강을 걱정해.

14. He should not eat (many / lots of) salt. 그는 많은 소금을 먹어서는 안 돼.

15. He asked (much / lots of) questions about her American life.
그는 그녀의 미국 생활에 대해 많은 질문들을 했어.

16. We took (many / much) photos. 우리는 많은 사진들을 찍었어.

17. The world has (much / lots of) lessons to teach him.
세상은 그에게 가르쳐줄 많은 교훈들을 가지고 있어요.

18. They learn (many / much) languages. 그들은 많은 언어들을 배워.

19. You shouldn't drink too (many / much) coffee.
너는 너무 많은 커피를 마셔서는 안 돼.

20. She could see (much / a lot of) people at the stadium.
그녀는 경기장에서 많은 사람들을 볼 수 있었어.

정답과 해설 p.4

UNIT 03 I eat a few doughnuts.

a few와 a little

앞에서 수량의 많음을 표현하는 many, much, a lot of, lots of를 배웠어요.
그렇다면 적음을 나타내고 싶을 때는 어떤 표현을 쓸까요?

❖ POiNT 1 ❖

a few 셀 수 있는 명사의 복수형 앞에 와요.

a few dogs
(강아지 몇 마리)

a few toys
(장난감 몇 개)

a few doughnuts
(도넛 몇 개)

I eat a few doughnuts. 나는 도넛 몇 개를 먹어.

조금일지라도 2개 이상이므로, a few 뒤에 있는 명사에는 -(e)s를 붙여야 해요.

❖ POiNT 2 ❖

a little 셀 수 없는 명사 앞에 와요.

a little work
(일 조금)

a little money
(돈 조금)

a little water
(물 조금)

He saved a little money. 그는 돈을 조금 모았어.

a little과 함께 쓰이는 명사는 셀 수 없는 명사이므로 뒤에 -(e)s를 붙여서는 안 돼요.

Check and Write

A 다음 빈칸에 a few와 a little 중 알맞은 것을 쓰세요.

1. 

[a few] balls

2. 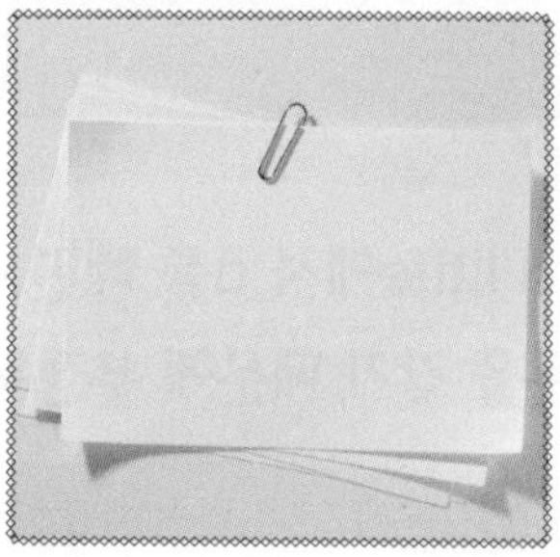

[ ] paper

3. 

[ ] cups

4. 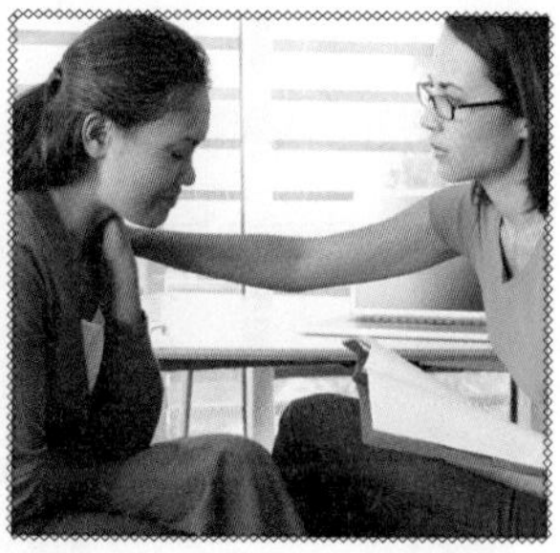

[ ] advice

5. 

[ ] mushrooms

6. 

[ ] spark

B 다음 ( )에서 알맞은 표현에 동그라미하고, 전체 문장을 다시 쓰세요.

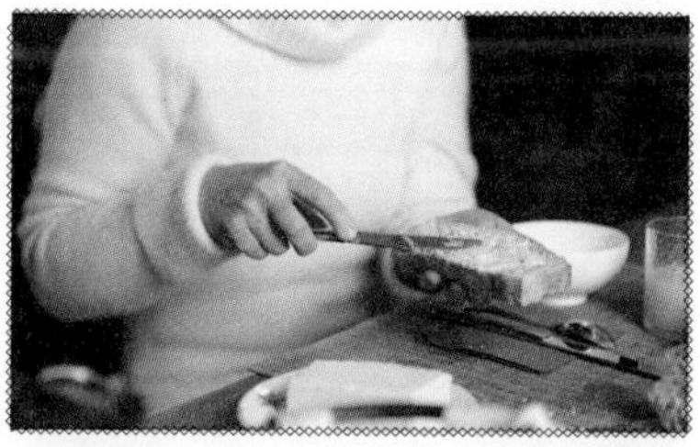

1. She puts (a few / a little) butter on bread.

➔ She puts a little butter on bread.

그녀는 빵에 버터 조금을 바른다.

2. I ordered a few (food / dishes).

➔ ________________________________.

나는 몇 개의 요리를 주문했다.

3. I just have a little (money / coins).

➔ ________________________________.

나는 단지 조금의 돈을 가지고 있다.

정답과 해설 p.4

UNIT

few와 little

04 I can see few flowers.

수량의 적음을 표현하는 a few와 a little에서 a를 빼면 뜻이 완전히 달라진답니다.
few와 little은 '거의 없는'이라는 뜻을 갖기 때문에 부정문처럼 해석돼요.

❖ POiNT 1 ❖

few 셀 수 있는 명사의 복수형 앞에 와요.

few flowers
(거의 없는 꽃)

few potatoes
(거의 없는 감자)

few pencils
(거의 없는 연필)

I can see few flowers. 나는 꽃을 거의 볼 수 없어.

❖ POiNT 2 ❖

little 셀 수 없는 명사 앞에 와요.

little rice
(거의 없는 쌀)

little cloud
(거의 없는 구름)

little milk
(거의 없는 우유)

I can see little cloud. 나는 구름을 거의 볼 수 없어.

Check and Write

A 다음 빈칸에 few와 little 중 알맞은 것을 쓰세요.

1. 

little juice

2. 

______ oil

3. 

______ desks

4. 

______ coins

5. 

______ leaves

6. 

______ time

B 다음 (　)에서 알맞은 것에 동그라미하고, 문장을 다시 쓰세요.

1. She has few (friend / friends).

→ She has few friends.

그녀는 친구가 거의 없다.

2. He drinks (few / little) water.

→ ______________________.

그는 물을 거의 마시지 않아.

3. My sister ate little (cake / piece of cake).

→ ______________________.

내 여동생은 케이크를 거의 먹지 않았다.

정답과 해설 p.4

Practice 1 적음을 표현하는 수량형용사의 쓰임을 익혀 보아요.

[A-C] 다음 빈칸에 들어갈 말로 적절한 것을 보기 에서 골라 쓰세요. (중복 사용 가능)

보기 a few a little few little

A Having fun!

1. I read ___a few___ books.
나는 책 몇 권을 읽었어.

2. I finished ____________ homework. 나는 숙제 조금을 끝냈어.

3. I have ____________ homework now. 나는 이제 숙제가 거의 없어.

4. I have ____________ time now. 이제 나는 시간이 조금 있어.

5. ____________ friends live here. 몇 명의 친구들이 여기에 살아.

6. They have ____________ work. 그들은 일이 조금 있어.

7. They had ____________ time. 그들은 시간이 거의 없었어.

8. I play games for ____________ hours.
나는 몇 시간 동안 게임을 해.

정답과 해설 p.4

B In the refrigerator

1. I need ______________ onions. 나는 양파 몇 개가 필요해.

2. Sihu drinks ______________ milk. 시후는 약간의 우유를 마셔.

3. He drinks ______________ water. 그는 물을 거의 마시지 않아.

4. We eat ______________ candies. 우리는 사탕을 거의 먹지 않아.

5. I use ______________ eggs. 나는 계란 몇 개를 사용해.

C I made fried rice!

1. I needed ______________ sugar. 나는 설탕이 조금 필요했어.

2. I put ______________ salt in the soup.
   나는 수프에 소금을 조금 넣었어.

3. I cut ______________ vegetables. 나는 야채 몇 개를 썰었어.

4. I fried ______________ meat. 나는 조금의 고기를 볶았어.

5. There was ______________ rice. 밥이 거의 없었어.

6. There were ______________ instant noodles. 라면이 거의 없었어.

7. I drank ______________ milk. 나는 약간의 우유를 마셨어.

정답과 해설 p.4

Practice 2 수량형용사의 알맞은 쓰임을 익혀 보아요.

다음 (   )에서 알맞은 것에 동그라미 하세요.

1. 

I have (few / little) clothes.
나는 옷이 거의 없어요.

2. 

I eat (few / little) meat.
나는 고기를 거의 먹지 않아요.

3. This flower needs (a few / a little) sunlight.
이 꽃은 약간의 햇빛이 필요해.

4. She has (a few / a little) money.
그녀는 약간의 돈이 있어.

5. He eats (a few / a little) meat.
그는 고기를 조금 먹어요.

6. We eat (a little / little) pepper.
우리는 후추를 거의 먹지 않아.

7. I have (few / a few) troubles.
나는 문제가 조금 있어요.

정답과 해설 p.4

8. They have (few / a few) cousins.
그들은 사촌이 거의 없어.

9. We need (a few / a little) salt.
우리는 조금의 소금이 필요해.

10.

I drank (a few / a little) milk this morning.
나는 오늘 아침 조금의 우유를 마셨어.

11.

They do (little / a little) exercise in winter.
그들은 겨울에는 거의 운동을 하지 않아.

12. You can see (little / a little) cloud in the sky.
당신은 하늘에서 구름을 거의 볼 수 없어요.

13. I read (few / a few) books.
나는 책을 거의 읽지 않아.

14. She drinks (little / a little) coffee at night.
그녀는 밤에 커피를 거의 마시지 않아.

정답과 해설 p.4

15.

I have (little / a little) homework.

나는 숙제가 조금 있어.

16.

She eats (few / a few) vegetables.

그녀는 야채를 거의 먹지 않아요.

17. I have (few / a few) hobbies.

나는 취미가 몇 개 있어.

18.

She has (few / a few) oranges.

그녀는 오렌지 몇 개를 갖고 있어.

19.

You have (few / little) time.

너는 시간이 거의 없어.

20. I have (few / little) salt.

나는 소금을 거의 가지고 있지 않아.

정답과 해설 p.4

Practice 3 수량형용사가 쓰인 문장을 완성해 보아요.

다음 우리말 뜻과 같도록 주어진 표현을 순서에 맞게 배열하여 문장을 완성하세요.
(단, 수량형용사는 반드시 명사 앞에 오도록 배열하세요.)

1. (a little, Give me, chocolate).
나에게 조금의 초콜릿을 줘.

→ Give me a little chocolate.

2. (candies, a few, has, She).
그녀는 사탕 몇 개가 있어.

→ ______________________.

3. (a few, I have, bananas).
나는 바나나 몇 개가 있어.

→ ______________________.

4. (is not harmful, chocolate, A little). 조금의 초콜릿은 해롭지 않아.

→ ______________________.

5. (kilos, a few, I, put on). 나는 살이 몇 킬로그램 쪘어.

→ ______________________.

6. (a few, I lost, kilos). 나는 살이 몇 킬로그램 빠졌어.

→ ______________________.

정답과 해설 p.4

7. (a few, I have, friends). 나는 몇 명의 친구가 있어.

➔ ______________________________.

8. (a little, She, bread, bought).
그녀는 빵을 조금 샀어.

➔ ______________________________
______________________________.

9. (I read, books, a few).
나는 책 몇 권을 읽었어.

➔ ______________________________
______________________________.

10. (little, He, drinks, Coke). 그는 콜라를 거의 마시지 않아.

➔ ______________________________.

11. (read, few, They, books). 그들은 책을 거의 읽지 않아.

➔ ______________________________.

12. (a little, did, I, homework). 나는 숙제를 조금 했어.

➔ ______________________________.

13. (Spanish, speak, I, a little). 나는 스페인어를 조금 해요.

➔ ______________________________.

정답과 해설 p.4

14. (eat, vegetables, few, I). 나는 야채를 거의 먹지 않아.

➔ ____.

15. (Dad, little, has, time). 아빠는 시간이 거의 없어요.

➔ ____.

16. (I, few, have, friends).

나는 친구가 거의 없어.

➔ ____________________

____________________.

17. (are, students, A few) in the classroom. 몇 명의 학생들이 교실에 있다.

➔ ____________________

in the classroom.

18. (little, together, time, We spent). 우리는 함께 보낸 시간이 거의 없었어요.

➔ ____.

19. (close friends, A few, live here). 몇 명의 절친한 친구들이 여기에 산다.

➔ ____.

20. (a little, Let me give you, advice). (*advice: 조언, 충고)

너에게 조언을 조금 할게.

➔ ____.

정답과 해설 p.4

Let's Practice More!

SET 01

학습목표 1 | a few와 a little을 비교해 보아요. 공부한 날 : 맞은 개수 : /12개

다음 ( ) 안에서 알맞은 표현을 골라보세요.

01. I ordered (a few / a little) dishes.
나는 요리 몇 개를 주문했어.

02. I ordered (a few / a little) food.
나는 음식 조금을 주문했어.

03. She put (a few / a little) salt in the soup.
그녀는 수프에 소금을 조금 넣었어.

04. He needs (a few / a little) onions.
그는 양파 몇 개가 필요해.

05. She has (a few / a little) hobbies.
그녀는 취미 몇 개가 있어.

06. Give me (a few / a little) chocolate.
나에게 초콜릿 조금을 줘.

07. My mom bought (a few / a little) bread.
나의 엄마는 빵 조금을 사셨어.

08. He has (a few / a little) homework.
그는 숙제 조금을 가지고 있어.

09. They have (a few / a little) bananas.
그들은 바나나 몇 개를 가지고 있어.

10. We need (a few / a little) sugar.
우리는 설탕 조금이 필요해.

11. She uses (a few / a little) eggs.
그녀는 계란 몇 개를 사용해.

12. Let me give you (a few / a little) advice.
너에게 조언을 조금 할게.

정답과 해설 p.4

Let's Practice More!

SET 02

학습목표 1 | a few와 a little을 비교해 보아요. 공부한 날 : 맞은 개수 : /14개

다음 문장의 빈칸에 a few나 a little 중 알맞은 것을 쓰세요.

01. I have ___a few___ mushrooms. 나는 버섯 몇 개를 가지고 있어.

02. My brother eats ________ meat. 나의 남동생은 고기를 조금 먹어요.

03. He plays games for ________ hours. 그는 몇 시간 동안 게임을 해.

04. They read ________ books. 그들은 책 몇 권을 읽었어.

05. You drank ________ milk. 너는 약간의 우유를 마셨어.

06. She cut ________ vegetables. 그녀는 야채 몇 개를 썰었어.

07. We have ________ time now. 이제 우리는 시간이 조금 있어.

08. My dad speaks ________ Spanish. 나의 아빠는 스페인어를 조금 하셔요.

09. We have ________ candies. 우리는 사탕 몇 개가 있어.

10. My mom fried ________ meat. 나의 엄마는 조금의 고기를 볶으셨어.

11. ________ close friends live here.
몇 명의 절친한 친구들이 여기에 산다.

12. He lost ________ kilos. 그는 살이 몇 킬로그램 빠졌어.

13. ________ chocolate is not harmful. 조금의 초콜릿은 해롭지 않아.

14. ________ students are in the classroom. 몇 명의 학생들이 교실에 있다.

정답과 해설 p.4

Let's Practice More!

SET 03

학습목표 2 | few와 little을 비교해 보아요.　　　공부한 날 :　　　맞은 개수 :　　/14개

다음 (　) 안에서 알맞은 단어를 골라보세요.

01. I have (few / little) friends. 나는 친구가 거의 없어.

02. We spent (few / little) time together. 우리는 함께 보낸 시간이 거의 없었어요.

03. We have (few / little) cousins. 우리는 사촌이 거의 없어.

04. He eats (few / little) pepper. 그는 후추를 거의 먹지 않아.

05. She drinks (few / little) coffee at night. 그녀는 밤에 커피를 거의 마시지 않아.

06. They have (few / little) time. 그들은 시간이 거의 없어.

07. My sister eats (few / little) candies. 나의 언니는 사탕을 거의 먹지 않아.

08. You have (few / little) clothes. 너는 옷이 거의 없어.

09. There were (few / little) instant noodles. 라면이 거의 없었어.

10. I have (few / little) homework now. 나는 이제 숙제가 거의 없어.

11. We can see (few / little) cloud in the sky.
우리는 하늘에서 구름을 거의 볼 수 없어요.

12. There was (few / little) rice. 쌀이 거의 없었어.

13. She does (few / little) exercise in winter.
그녀는 겨울에 운동을 거의 하지 않아.

14. You have (few / little) work. 너는 일이 거의 없어.

정답과 해설 p.5

Let's Practice More!

SET 04

학습목표 2 | few와 little을 비교해 보아요. 공부한 날 : 맞은 개수 : /12개

다음 문장의 빈칸에 few나 little 중 알맞은 것을 쓰세요.

01. I have ___little___ time. 나는 시간이 거의 없어.

02. My brother eats ________ vegetables.
나의 남동생은 야채를 거의 먹지 않아.

03. She has ________ salt. 그녀는 소금을 거의 가지고 있지 않아.

04. He drinks ________ Coke. 그는 콜라를 거의 마시지 않아.

05. There was ________ sugar. 설탕이 거의 없었어.

06. My sister has ________ friends. 나의 여동생은 친구가 거의 없어.

07. She has ________ oranges. 그녀는 오렌지를 거의 가지고 있지 않아.

08. My grandmother drinks ________ water. 나의 할머니는 물을 거의 마시지 않으셔.

09. We have ________ rice. 우리는 쌀을 거의 가지고 있지 않아.

10. They have ________ troubles. 그들은 문제가 거의 없어.

11. My dad drinks ________ coffee at night. 나의 아빠는 밤에 커피를 거의 마시지 않으셔.

12. ________ students are in the classroom.
교실에 학생들이 거의 없어.

정답과 해설 p.5

Let's Practice More!

SET 05

학습목표 3 | a few와 few를 비교해 보아요. 공부한 날 : 맞은 개수 : /14개

다음 문장이 우리말 해석과 같은 뜻이 되도록 ( ) 안에서 알맞은 표현을 골라보세요.

01. This store sells (a few / few) shoes. 이 상점은 조금의 신발을 판다.

02. This store sells (a few / few) shoes. 이 상점은 신발을 거의 팔지 않는다.

03. My mom uses (a few / few) eggs. 나의 엄마는 계란을 거의 사용하지 않으셔.

04. My mom uses (a few / few) eggs.
나의 엄마는 계란 몇 개를 사용하셔.

05. He has (a few / few) cousins. 그는 사촌이 몇 명 있어.

06. He has (a few / few) cousins. 그는 사촌이 거의 없어.

07. We read (a few / few) books. 우리는 책 몇 권을 읽었어.

08. We read (a few / few) books. 우리는 책을 거의 읽지 않았어.

09. (A few / Few) friends live here. 여기에 친구들이 거의 살지 않아.

10. (A few / Few) friends live here. 몇 명의 친구들이 여기에 살아.

11. They cut (a few / few) vegetables. 그들은 야채 몇 개를 썰었어.

12. They cut (a few / few) vegetables. 그들은 야채를 거의 썰지 않았어.

13. She needs (a few / few) onions. 그녀는 양파 몇 개가 필요해.

14. She needs (a few / few) onions. 그녀는 양파가 거의 필요하지 않아.

정답과 해설 p.5

Let's Practice More!

SET 06

학습목표 4 | a little과 little을 비교해 보아요.　　공부한 날 :　　맞은 개수 :　　/14개

CH 02

다음 문장이 우리말 해석과 같은 뜻이 되도록 (　) 안에서 알맞은 표현을 골라보세요.

01. We spent (a little / little) time together.
우리는 함께 약간의 시간을 보냈다.

02. This flower needs (a little / little) sunlight.
이 꽃은 약간의 햇빛이 필요해.

03. I had (a little / little) money. 나는 돈이 거의 없었다.

04. Let me give you (a little / little) advice. 너에게 조언을 조금 할게.

05. He did (a little / little) homework. 그는 숙제를 거의 하지 않았다.

06. Give him (a little / little) chocolate. 그에게 조금의 초콜릿을 줘.

07. We can see (a little / little) cloud in the sky.
우리는 하늘에서 구름을 거의 볼 수 없어요.

08. (A little / Little) Coke is not harmful. 조금의 콜라는 해롭지 않아.

09. She speaks (a little / little) English. 그녀는 영어를 거의 하지 못해요.

10. They bought (a little / little) bread. 그들은 빵을 조금 샀어.

11. I need (a little / little) salt. 나는 조금의 소금이 필요해.

12. She had (a little / little) time. 그녀는 시간이 거의 없었어.

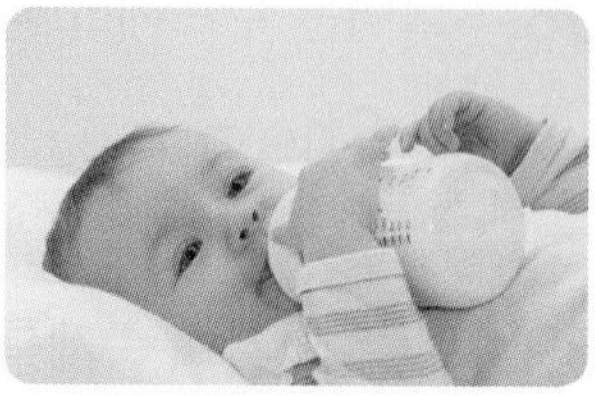

13. The baby drinks (a little / little) milk. 그 아기는 약간의 우유를 마셔.

14. He finished (a little / little) homework. 그는 숙제를 거의 끝내지 못했다.

정답과 해설 p.5

Let's Practice More!

SET 07

학습목표 5 | a few, a little, few, little의 쓰임을 익혀 보아요. 공부한 날 : 맞은 개수 : /20개

우리말 뜻과 같도록 ( ) 안의 단어를 이용하여 문장을 완성하세요.

01.

그는 사탕 몇 개가 있어. (candies)

→ He has a few candies ______________.

02.

나의 엄마는 양파 몇 개를 썰었어. (onions)

→ My mom cut ______________.

03. 나는 빵이 조금 필요해요. (bread)

→ I need ______________.

04. 나의 남동생은 취미가 몇 개 있어. (hobbies)

→ My brother has ______________.

05. 그들은 함께 보낸 시간이 거의 없었어요. (time)

→ They spent ______________ together.

06. 우리는 사촌이 거의 없어. (cousins)

→ We have ______________.

07. 그들은 몇 시간 동안 게임을 해. (hours)

→ They play games for ______________.

08. 그녀는 수프에 소금을 조금 넣었어. (salt)

→ She put ______________ in the soup.

09. 그는 약간의 숙제를 끝냈어. (homework)

→ He finished ______________.

정답과 해설 p.5

10. 

그녀는 친구가 거의 없어. (friends)

→ She has ______________
______________________.

11. 

몇 명의 학생들이 교실에 있다. (students)

→ ______________________
are in the classroom.

12. 나의 아빠는 고기를 거의 드시지 않아. (meat)

→ My dad eats ______________________________.

13. 나는 바나나 몇 개를 샀다. (bananas)

→ I bought ______________________________.

14. 그들은 설탕이 조금 필요했다. (sugar)

→ They needed ______________________________.

15. 나는 물을 거의 마시지 않아. (water)

→ I drink ______________________________.

16. 그는 살이 몇 킬로그램 빠졌어. (kilos)

→ He lost ______________________________.

17. 우리는 문제가 거의 없다. (troubles)

→ We have ______________________________.

18. 그들은 야채를 거의 사지 않았어. (vegetables)

→ They bought ______________________________.

19. 그녀는 오늘 아침 조금의 우유를 마셨어. (milk)

→ She drank ______________________ this morning.

20. 그는 책을 거의 읽지 않았어. (books)

→ He read ______________________________.

정답과 해설 p.5

Let's Practice More!

SET 08

학습목표 5 | a few, a little, few, little의 쓰임을 익혀 보아요. 공부한 날 : 맞은 개수 : /20개

다음 문장이 우리말 해석과 같은 뜻이 되도록 빈칸을 완성해 보세요.

01. 

This store sells a few shoes ______________.

이 상점은 조금의 신발을 판다.

02. 

This flower needs ______________ ______________.

이 꽃은 약간의 물이 필요해.

03. There were ______________.

오렌지가 거의 없었어.

04. We have ______________ now.

우리는 이제 숙제가 거의 없어.

05. They have ______________.

그들은 돈을 거의 가지고 있지 않아.

06. My sister eats ______________.

나의 여동생은 사탕 몇 개를 먹는다.

07. They spent ______________ together.

그들은 약간의 시간을 함께 보냈어요.

08. There was ______________.

초콜릿이 거의 없었어.

09. She has ______________.

그녀는 옷이 거의 없어요.

10. My uncle speaks ______________.

나의 삼촌은 한국어를 조금 해요.

정답과 해설 p.5

11.

Sihu drinks ___________

______________________.

시후는 약간의 콜라를 마셔.

12.

I drank ______________

this morning.

나는 오늘 아침 조금의 커피를 마셨어.

13. He read ______________________________________.

그는 몇 권의 책을 읽었어.

14. You can see ______________________________________ in winter.

당신은 겨울에 꽃을 거의 볼 수 없어요.

15. He does ______________________________________ at night.

그는 밤에는 거의 운동을 하지 않아.

16. ______________________________________ live here.

몇 명의 친구들이 여기에 산다.

17. She put on ______________________________________.

그녀는 살이 몇 킬로그램 쪘어.

18. My grandmother fried ____________________________.

나의 할머니는 조금의 고기를 볶으셨어.

19. He uses ______________________________________.

그는 계란을 거의 사용하지 않아.

20. They have ______________________________________.

그들은 일이 거의 없어.

정답과 해설 p.5

UNIT

05 I want to drink some water.

some과 any

많지는 않지만 일일이 세기는 애매할 때 '약간의' '몇몇의' '어느 정도'라고 표현하죠.
이렇게 대략적인 수나 양을 표현하는 단어에는 some과 any가 있어요.

❖ POiNT 1 ❖

some과 any 뒤에는 셀 수 있는 명사와 셀 수 없는 명사가 모두 올 수 있기 때문에 some과 any는 뒤에 오는 명사만으로는 용법의 차이를 구분할 수 없어요.
대신 둘은 서로 쓰이는 문장이 달라서 문장 전체를 보고 구분해야 해요!

❖ POiNT 2 ❖

some

부정문과 의문문보다는 주로 긍정문에 쓰여요.

긍정문	I want to drink some water. 나는 약간의 물을 마시고 싶어.

그렇다면 some은 의문문에는 전혀 쓸 수 없는 걸까요? 그건 아니에요!
누군가에게 무언가를 권하거나 요청하는 의문문일 때에는 some을 써야 해요.

권유 의문문	Would you like some water? 물 좀 마실래?
요청 의문문	Can I get some water? 물 좀 마셔도 될까?

any

긍정문보다는 부정문과 의문문에 쓰여요.

부정문	I don't have any money. 난 돈이 조금도 없어.
의문문	Do you have any books? 너 책 좀 가지고 있어?

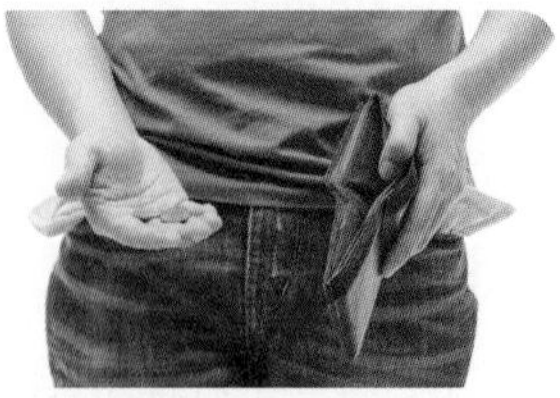

그렇다면 any는 긍정문에는 전혀 쓸 수 없는 걸까요?
any가 긍정문에서 쓰이면 '어떤 ~라도'라는 뜻이 돼요.

긍정문	Any child can learn English. 어떤 아이라도 영어를 배울 수 있어.

Check and Write

A 우리말 뜻을 참고하여 some과 any 중에서 알맞은 것을 쓰고, 문장을 다시 쓰세요.

1. Mr. Kim, I have ___some___ questions.
김 선생님, 저 질문이 좀 있어요.
➔ ___Mr. kim, I have some questions___.

2. Can I ask __________ questions?
제가 질문을 좀 해도 될까요?
➔ ______________________________?

3. Do you have __________ questions?
질문들이 좀 있으신가요?
➔ ______________________________?

B 우리말 뜻을 참고하여 다음 (　)에서 알맞은 것에 동그라미 하고, 문장을 다시 쓰세요.

1. Would you like (some / any) popcorn?
당신은 팝콘을 좀 드시겠어요?
➔ ___Would you like some popcorn___?

2. I don't need (some / any) help.
저는 조금의 도움도 필요 없어요.
➔ ______________________________.

3. (Some / Any) people think he is crazy.
몇몇 사람들은 그가 미쳤다고 생각해요.
➔ ______________________________.

정답과 해설 p.5

UNIT

06 All students go to school every day.

all과 every

'모두' '전체'를 표현하고 싶을 때는 all과 every를 써요.

❖ POiNT 1 ❖

all은 셀 수 있는 명사의 복수형 / 셀 수 없는 명사와 함께 쓰여요.

All students go to school every day. 모든 학생들은 매일 학교에 간다.

I lost all my money on the train. 나는 기차에서 내 모든 돈을 잃어버렸어.

all 뒤에 오는 셀 수 있는 명사는 반드시 복수명사로 쓰고, 셀 수 없는 명사는 반드시 단수명사로 써요. 「all + 셀 수 있는 명사의 복수」가 주어로 쓰이면, 반드시 복수동사를 쓰고, 「all + 셀 수 없는 명사」가 주어로 쓰이면, 반드시 단수동사를 써요. all과 명사 사이에 정관사 the나 소유격이 쓰이기도 해요.

all apples

all my friends

all the time

❖ POiNT 2 ❖

every는 항상 단수명사와 쓰여요.

Every student needs a pencil. 모든 학생들은 연필이 필요하다.

every는 '모든'이라고 해석되어 뒤에 복수명사가 올 것 같지만, 항상 뒤에 단수 명사가 온다는 것을 꼭 외워두세요! Every student는 단수 주어이기 때문에 단수동사(needs)가 쓰였어요.

all students (전체로서 모두)

every student (하나하나 모두)

Check and Write

A 다음 빈칸에 all과 every 중 알맞은 단어를 넣어보세요.

1. 

[all] pencils

2. 

[ ] house

3. 

[ ] onions

4. 

[ ] day

5. 

[ ] monkey

6. 

[ ] my friends

B 알맞은 단어에 동그라미 하세요.

1. 

all the (person / people)

2. 

every (month / months)

3. 

Every seat (is / are) empty.

4. 

All the babies (is / are) cute.

정답과 해설 p.5

Practice 1 수량형용사의 쓰임을 익혀 보아요.

[A–D]우리말 뜻을 참고하여 다음 보기 에서 알맞은 단어를 골라 빈칸에 써 보세요. (중복 사용 가능)

A What do you want?

보기 some any

1. Would you like ___some___ cookies? They're yummy.
   너 쿠키 좀 먹을래? 그것들은 맛있어.

2. I don't want ______________ sweets.
   나는 단 것들을 조금도 원하지 않아.

3. Can I drink ______________ milk?
   내가 우유를 좀 먹어도 될까?

4. I want to have ______________ cold water.
   나 시원한 물을 좀 먹고 싶어.

B Help my dog!

보기 some any

1. Do you have ______________ pets?
   너 애완동물 키워?

2. My dog wants ______________ raw meat.
   내 강아지는 생고기를 좀 원해.

3. Is there ______________ problem?
   무슨 문제없어?

4. I can't find ______________ problem.
   나는 문제를 조금도 찾지 못했는데.

5. Buy ______________ healthy food for your dog.
   너의 강아지를 위해 건강한 사료를 좀 사.

정답과 해설 p.5

C Drawing pictures

보기 all[All] every

1. Do you paint ___________ day?
너 매일 그림 그리는 거야?

2. I paint ___________ Saturday.
나는 매주 토요일마다 그림을 그려.

3. ___________ my paintings are beautiful.
나의 모든 그림들은 아름다워.

4. ___________ teachers praised me for my picture. (*praise: 칭찬하다)
모든 선생님들이 내 그림을 칭찬해주셨어.

D Friends

보기 all has any some[Some] every

1. Everybody ___________ friends.
모두가 친구들을 가지고 있어.

2. They play with their friends ___________ day long.
그들은 하루 종일 그들의 친구들과 놀아.

3. But I don't have ___________ friends.
하지만 나는 친구가 한 명도 없어.

4. I walk to the park ___________ Sunday.
나는 매주 일요일에 공원으로 걸어 가.

5. ___________ kids are in the park.
몇 명의 아이들이 공원에 있어.

정답과 해설 p.5

Practice 2 수량형용사가 쓰인 문장을 완성해 보아요.

다음 우리말 뜻과 같도록 주어진 표현을 순서에 맞게 배열하여 문장을 완성하세요.

1. (didn't come, Some students, to school) today.
   몇몇 친구들이 오늘 학교에 안 왔어.
   ➔ Some students didn't come to school today.

2. (any, Did they have, problem with the car)?
   그들은 차에 문제가 좀 있었던 거야?
   ➔ ____________________?

3. (school buses, All, arrived late) this morning. 오늘 아침에 모든 스쿨버스가 늦게 왔대.
   ➔ ____________________ this morning.

4. (any, help, Do they need)? 그들에게 도움이 좀 필요할까?
   ➔ ____________________?

5. (any, Did you get, information)? 너는 정보를 좀 얻었니?
   ➔ ____________________?

6. Don't worry. (Everything, fine, will be). 걱정하지 마. 모든 것이 잘 될 거야.
   ➔ Don't worry. ____________________.

7. (money, Do you need, any)? 너는 돈이 좀 필요하니?
   ➔ ____________________?

8. (every, He doesn't work, Saturday).
   그는 매주 토요일에 일하지 않아.
   ➔ ____________________.

9. (some, We should find, solutions). 우리는 해결책을 좀 찾아야해.
   ➔ ____________________.

10. (have, idea, any, Do you)? 너 의견 좀 있어?
    ➔ ____________________?

정답과 해설 p.5

11. (questions, any, Did you ask)? 너는 질문들을 좀 했니?

➔ ____?

12. (comic books, some, Can you lend me)? 나에게 만화책 좀 빌려줄 수 있어요?

➔ ____?

13. (storybooks, any, I don't have). 나는 이야기책이 하나도 없어.

➔ ____.

14. (will come true, my dreams, All).
내 모든 꿈들이 이루어질 거야.

➔ ______________________________.

15. Heungbu : Dear brother, (some, can I, borrow, rice)?
흥부 : 형님, 제가 쌀을 좀 빌릴 수 있을까요?

➔ Dear brother, ______________________________?

16. (are, starving, my children, All). (*starve: 굶다)
나의 모든 자식들이 굶고 있어요.

➔ ____.

17. (cloud has, a silver lining, Every).
모든 구름은 은빛 테두리(구름 뒤 햇살)가 있다. (어려운 상황에도 희망은 있다.)

➔ ____.

18. (all, Time heals, wounds). 시간은 모든 상처를 치유한다. (시간이 약이다.) (*wounds: 상처)

➔ ____.

19. (all, Don't put, your eggs, in one basket).
너의 모든 달걀들을 한 바구니 안에 넣지 마라. (한 가지 일에 모든 것을 걸지 마라.)

➔ ____.

20. (garden may have, some, Every, weeds). (*weeds: 잡초)
모든 정원에는 어느 정도의 잡초가 있다. (모든 것에는 약점이 있다.)

➔ ____.

정답과 해설 p.5

Practice 3 알맞은 수량형용사를 쓸 수 있어요.

다음 밑줄 친 부분을 바르게 고쳐 전체 문장을 다시 쓰세요.

1. They gave her <u>any</u> good books.
그들은 그녀에게 좋은 책을 몇 권 주었다.

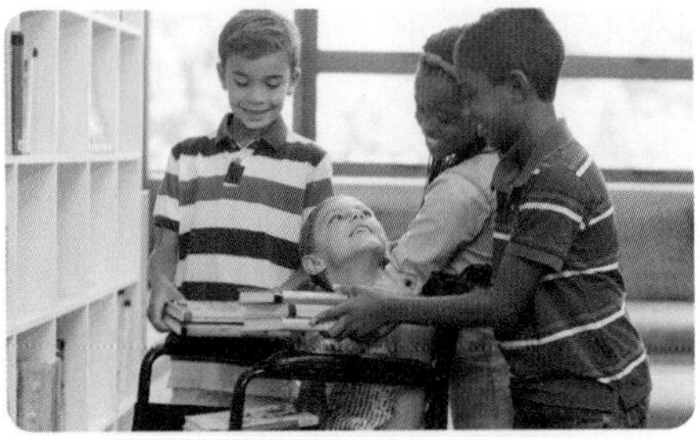

→ They gave her some good books.

2. I read <u>any</u> webtoons.
나는 웹툰 몇 개를 읽었어.

→ ______________________.

3. I read them <u>all</u> Sunday. 나는 그것들을 매주 일요일에 읽었어.

→ ______________________.

4. <u>Every</u> my friends love them, too! 내 모든 친구들도 그것들을 좋아하더라!

→ ______________________!

5. Every child <u>need</u> friends. 모든 아이들은 친구들이 필요해.

→ ______________________.

6. All dogs <u>is</u> children's best friends.
모든 개들은 아이들의 최고의 친구들이야.

→ ______________________.

7. But some children don't like <u>some</u> dogs.
하지만 몇몇 아이들은 강아지들을 조금도 좋아하지 않아.

→ ______________________.

8. I don't have <u>some</u> pets. 나는 애완동물을 하나도 가지고 있지 않아.

→ ______________________.

9. I want <u>any</u> pets. 나는 몇 마리의 애완동물들을 원해.

→ ______________________.

정답과 해설 p.6

10. Every Koreans eat rice. 모든 한국인들은 쌀을 먹어.

➔ ______________________________.

11. I don't eat some rice. 나는 쌀을 조금도 먹지 않아.

➔ ______________________________.

12. Any vegetables taste good. 몇몇 채소들은 맛있어.

➔ ______________________________.

13. No way! All vegetables tastes bad!
그럴 리가! 모든 채소들은 맛없어!

➔ ______________________________!

14. Do you have some questions? 질문들이 좀 있나요?

➔ ______________________________?

15. I asked any questions. 나는 질문 몇 개를 했어.

➔ ______________________________.

16. Every students passed the exam. 모든 학생들이 시험을 통과했어.

➔ ______________________________.

17. Would you like any ice cream?
너 아이스크림 좀 먹을래?

➔ ______________________________?

18. Can I have any Coke? 저 콜라 좀 먹어도 돼요?

➔ ______________________________?

19. I read two books all week. 나는 매주 두 권의 책을 읽었어.

➔ ______________________________.

20. Every mothers loves her daughter.
모든 엄마들은 그녀의 딸을 사랑해.

➔ ______________________________.

정답과 해설 p.6

Let's Practice More!

SET 01

학습목표 1 | some과 any의 쓰임을 구별할 수 있어요. 공부한 날 : 맞은 개수 : /12개

우리말 뜻을 참고하여 다음 ( )안에 알맞은 단어를 골라보세요.

01. I want (some / any) cookies. 나는 약간의 쿠키를 원해.

02. Would you like (some / any) tea? 차 좀 드시겠어요?

03. I don't need (some / any) help. 나는 조금의 도움도 필요 없어.

04. Can I drink (some / any) milk? 내가 우유를 좀 먹어도 될까?

05. Did they have (some / any) problem with the car?
그들은 차에 문제가 좀 있었던 거야?

06. (Some / Any) kids are in the park. 몇 명의 아이들이 공원에 있어.

07. I don't want (some / any) sweets. 나는 단 것들을 조금도 원하지 않아.

08. I don't have (some / any) friends. 나는 친구가 한 명도 없어.

09. (Some / Any) child can learn chinese. 어떤 아이라도 중국어를 배울 수 있어.

10. Do you have (some / any) idea? 너 의견 좀 있어?

11. Can you lend me (some / any) comic books?
나에게 만화책 좀 빌려줄 수 있어요?

12. I don't have (some / any) pets. 나는 애완동물을 하나도 가지고 있지 않아.

정답과 해설 p.6

Let's Practice More!

SET 02

학습목표 1 | some과 any의 쓰임을 구별할 수 있어요. 공부한 날 : 맞은 개수 : /14개

우리말 뜻을 참고하여 다음 문장의 빈칸에 some과 any 중 알맞은 것을 쓰세요.

01. I have ___some___ mushrooms. 나는 약간의 버섯이 있어.

02. I don't have __________ mushrooms.
나는 버섯을 조금도 갖고 있지 않아.

03. My dog wants __________ raw meat. 내 강아지는 생고기를 좀 원해.

04. I want to have __________ cold water. 나 시원한 물을 좀 먹고 싶어.

05. Do they need __________ help? 그들에게 도움이 좀 필요할까?

06. We read __________ webtoons. 우리는 웹툰 몇 개를 읽어.

07. I don't eat __________ rice. 나는 쌀을 조금도 먹지 않아.

08. They asked __________ questions. 그들은 질문 몇 개를 했어.

09. Can I have __________ cake? 저 케이크 좀 먹어도 돼요?

10. __________ vegetables taste good. 몇몇 채소들은 맛있어.

11. They don't have __________ storybooks. 그들은 이야기책이 하나도 없어.

12. Did you get __________ information? 너는 정보를 좀 얻었니?

13. Would you like __________ ice cream? 너 아이스크림 좀 먹을래?

14. Every garden may have __________ weeds.
모든 정원에는 어느 정도의 잡초가 있다. (모든 것에는 약점이 있다.)

정답과 해설 p.6

Let's Practice More!

SET 03

학습목표 2 | all과 명사 사이에는 정관사 the 또는 소유격이 들어갈 수 있음을 익혀 보아요.

공부한 날 :　　　　맞은 개수 :　　/14개

주어진 우리말 뜻을 보고 ( ) 안에 있는 단어들을 순서에 맞게 배열하여 문장을 완성해 보세요.

01. I read ___all the books___. (the, all, books)
나는 모든 책을 읽었어.

02. ________________ is stolen. (money, her, All)
그녀의 모든 돈이 도둑맞았어.

03. ________________ will come true. (dreams, my, All)
내 모든 꿈들이 이루어질 거야.

04. ________________ praised her for her picture. (All, teachers, the)
모든 선생님들이 그녀의 그림을 칭찬해주셨어.

05. ________________ are smiling. (her, All, friends)
그녀의 모든 친구들은 웃고 있어.

06. ________________ are beautiful. (paintings, my, All)
나의 모든 그림들은 아름다워.

07. He was tired ________________. (time, the, all)
그는 항상 피곤했어.

08. ________________ were perfect! (All, dishes, the)
모든 음식들이 완벽했어! (*dish: 음식, 요리)

09. ________________ are starving. (my, All, children)
나의 모든 자식들이 굶고 있어요.

10. ________________ are cute. (the, All, babies)
모든 아기들은 귀여워.

11. ________________ love them, too! (friends, my, All)
내 모든 친구들도 그것들을 좋아하더라!

12. ________________ are standing. (All, people, the)
모든 사람들이 서 있어.

13. She is kind ________________. (the, all, time)
그녀는 항상 친절해.

14. Don't put ________________ in one basket. (eggs, your, all)
너의 모든 달걀들을 한 바구니 안에 넣지 마라. (한 가지 일에 모든 것을 걸지 마라.)

정답과 해설 p.6

Let's Practice More!

SET 04

학습목표 3 | all과 every를 비교해 보아요. 　공부한 날 : 　맞은 개수 : /12개

다음 ( ) 안에서 알맞은 단어를 골라보세요.

01. I walk to the park (all / every) Sunday.
나는 매주 일요일에 공원으로 걸어 가.

02. I read them (all / every) Sunday.
나는 그것들을 매주 일요일에 읽어.

03. (All / Every) your dreams will come true.
너의 모든 꿈들은 이루어질 거야.

04. (All / Every) cloud has a silver lining.
모든 구름은 은빛 테두리(구름 뒤 햇살)가 있다. (어려운 상황에도 희망은 있다.)

05. (All / Every) child needs friends.
모든 아이들은 친구들이 필요해.

06. (All / Every) his children are starving.
그의 모든 자식들이 굶고 있어요.

07. (All / Every) teacher praised you.
모든 선생님들이 너를 칭찬하셨어.

08. (All / Every) passengers are sleeping.
모든 승객들이 자고 있어.

09. (All / Every) trains arrived on time.
모든 기차들이 제 시간에 도착했어.

10. (All / Every) father loves his children.
모든 아버지들은 그의 아이들을 사랑해.

11. She goes shopping (all / every) Saturday.
그녀는 매주 토요일에 쇼핑을 하러 가.

12. (All / Every) their songs are beautiful.
모든 그들의 노래들은 아름다워.

정답과 해설 p.6

Let's Practice More!

SET 05

학습목표 3 | all과 every를 비교해 보아요.　　공부한 날 :　　맞은 개수 :　　/14개

다음 문장의 빈칸에 all과 every중 알맞은 것을 쓰세요.

01. ___All___ passengers are sleeping. 모든 승객들이 자고 있어.

02. I read two books ________ week. 나는 매주 두 권의 책을 읽어.

03. ________ teachers praised me. 모든 선생님들이 나를 칭찬해주셨어.

04. He doesn't work ________ Saturday. 그는 매주 토요일에 일하지 않아.

05. ________ school buses arrived late this morning.
오늘 아침에 모든 스쿨버스가 늦게 왔어.

06. They paint ________ Sunday. 그들은 매주 일요일마다 그림을 그려.

07. ________ Koreans eat rice. 모든 한국인들은 쌀을 먹어.

08. ________ student passed the exam. 모든 학생들이 시험을 통과했어.

09. ________ vegetables taste bad! 모든 채소들은 맛없어!

10. ________ passenger is sleeping. 모든 승객들이 자고 있어.

11. ________ mother loves her daughter. 모든 엄마들은 그녀의 딸을 사랑해.

12. Time heals ________ wounds. 시간은 모든 상처를 치유한다. (시간이 약이다.)

13. ________ garden may have some weeds.
모든 정원에는 어느 정도의 잡초가 있다. (모든 것에는 약점이 있다.)

14. ________ my dreams will come true.
내 모든 꿈들이 이루어질 거야.

정답과 해설 p.6

Let's Practice More!

SET 06

학습목표 3 | all과 every를 비교해 보아요.　　공부한 날 :　　맞은 개수 :　　/14개

다음 ( ) 안에서 알맞은 단어를 골라보세요.

01. Everybody (have / has) friends.
모두가 친구들을 가지고 있어.

02. All dogs (is / are) children's best friends. 모든 개들은 아이들의 최고의 친구들이야.

03. Every cloud (have / has) a silver lining.
모든 구름은 은빛 테두리(구름 뒤 햇살)가 있다. (어려운 상황에도 희망은 있다.)

04. All vegetables (taste / tastes) bad! 모든 채소들은 맛없어!

05. Every child (need / needs) friends. 모든 아이들은 친구들이 필요해.

06. All my friends (love / loves) them, too! 내 모든 친구들도 그것들을 좋아해!

07. All Japanese (eat / eats) rice. 모든 일본인들은 쌀을 먹어.

08. Every mother (love / loves) her son. 모든 엄마들은 그녀의 아들을 사랑해.

09. Every student (pass / passes) the exam. 모든 학생들이 시험을 통과해.

10. All his songs (is / are) beautiful. 그의 모든 노래들은 아름다워.

11. Every seat (is / are) empty. 모든 좌석이 비어있어.

12. Every teacher (praise / praises) her.
모든 선생님들이 그녀를 칭찬해.

13. All students (dance / dances).
모든 학생들이 춤을 춰.

14. Every passenger (sleep / sleeps). 모든 승객들이 잠을 자.

정답과 해설 p.6

Let's Practice More!

SET 07

학습목표 4 | some, any를 더 공부해 보아요.   공부한 날 :   맞은 개수 : /20개

다음 문장이 우리말 해석과 같은 뜻이 되도록 ( )안에 주어진 단어를 사용해서 빈칸을 완성해 보세요.

01.

I asked some questions.

(questions) 나는 질문 몇 개를 했어.

02.

Can I have ______________?

(Coke) 저 콜라 좀 먹어도 돼요?

03. Can you lend me ______________? (books)

나에게 책 몇 권을 빌려 줄 수 있니?

04. I don't need ______________. (help)

나는 조금의 도움도 필요하지 않아요.

05. I don't eat ______________. (rice)

나는 조금의 쌀도 먹지 않아.

06. Do you have ______________? (pets)

너 애완동물 키워?

07. I don't have ______________. (pets)

나는 애완동물들을 하나도 가지고 있지 않아.

08. Can I borrow ______________? (rice)

제가 쌀을 좀 빌릴 수 있을까요?

09. I don't have ______________. (storybooks)

나는 이야기책을 하나도 갖고 있지 않아.

정답과 해설 p.6

10. 

_______________ taste good.
(vegetables) 몇몇 채소들은 맛있어.

11. 

I want _______________.
(pets) 나는 몇 마리의 애완동물을 원해.

12. Is there ______________________________? (problem)
무슨 문제있어?

13. I can't find ______________________________. (problems)
나는 문제를 조금도 찾을 수가 없어.

14. Buy ______________________________ for your dog. (healthy food)
너의 강아지를 위해 건강한 사료를 좀 사.

15. ______________________________ didn't come to school today. (students)
몇몇 학생들이 오늘 학교에 안 왔어.

16. Do you have ______________________________? (idea)
너 의견 좀 있어?

17. They gave him ______________________________. (books)
그들은 그에게 책을 몇 권 주었다.

18. ______________________________ don't like dogs. (children)
몇몇 아이들은 개들을 좋아하지 않아.

19. ______________________________ can learn English. (child)
어떤 아이라도 영어를 배울 수 있어.

20. Would you like ______________________________? (cookies)
너 쿠키 좀 먹을래?

정답과 해설 p.6

Let's Practice More!

SET 08

학습목표 5 | every, all을 더 공부해 보아요. 공부한 날 : 맞은 개수 : /20개

다음 밑줄 친 부분이 맞으면 ○, 틀리면 고쳐 써 보세요.

01.

Every seat <u>are</u> empty.
모든 좌석이 비어있어.
→ is

02.

<u>All</u> the babies are cute.
모든 아기들은 귀여워.
→ ______

03. Every <u>children</u> needs friends. → ______
모든 아이들은 친구들이 필요해.

04. All school <u>bus</u> arrived late this morning. → ______
오늘 아침에 모든 스쿨버스가 늦게 왔대.

05. All my <u>dream</u> will come true. → ______
모든 내 꿈들이 이루어질 거야.

06. Every <u>garden</u> may have some weeds. → ______
모든 정원에는 어느 정도의 잡초가 있다. (모든 것에는 약점이 있다.)

07. All <u>Koreans</u> eat rice. → ______
모든 한국인들은 쌀을 먹어.

08. Every <u>student</u> passed the exam. → ______
모든 학생들이 시험을 통과했어.

09. All teachers <u>praises</u> him. → ______
모든 선생님들이 그를 칭찬해.

정답과 해설 p.6

10.

Every mother love her daughter.

→ ______________________

모든 엄마들은 그녀의 딸을 사랑해.

11.

Do you paint every days?

→ ______________________

너 매일 그림 그리니?

12. Every cloud have a silver lining. → ______________________

모든 구름은 은빛 테두리(구름 뒤 햇살)가 있다. (어려운 상황에도 희망은 있다.)

13. All dogs are children's best friends. → ______________________

모든 개들은 아이들의 최고의 친구들이야.

14. Time heals all wounds. → ______________________

시간은 모든 상처를 치유한다. (시간이 약이다.)

15. All my painting are beautiful. → ______________________

나의 모든 그림들은 아름다워.

16. I read three books every weeks. → ______________________

나는 매주 세 권의 책을 읽어.

17. All vegetables taste bad! → ______________________

모든 채소들은 맛없어!

18. All the people like him. → ______________________

모든 사람들이 그를 좋아해.

19. We work every Saturdays. → ______________________

우리는 매주 토요일마다 일해.

20. Everybody have friends. → ______________________

모두가 친구들을 가지고 있어.

정답과 해설 p.6

실전테스트

CHAPTER 01~02

공부한 날 :

복습한 날 :

부모님 확인 :

CHAPTER 01 부가의문문 CHAPTER 02 수량형용사

● 정답과 해설은 별책 7쪽에서 확인하세요!!

01

다음 밑줄 친 부분이 어색한 것을 고르세요.

① I have little soap.
② She doesn't have much time today.
③ Do you have any problems?
④ I don't want some milk.

[02~05] 다음 그림을 보고, 빈칸에 들어갈 알맞은 말을 [보기]에서 골라 쓰세요.

[보기] many a lot of little few

02

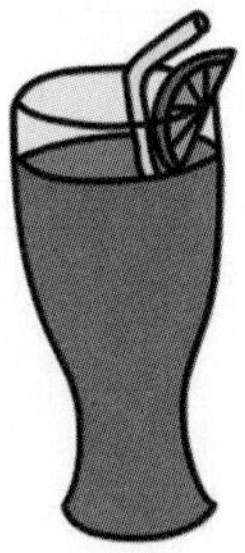

I have __________ orange juice.

03

There are __________ toys in the box.

04

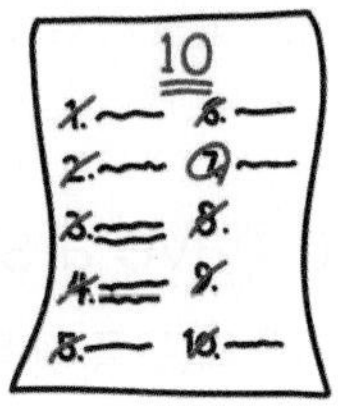

He got __________ correct answers.

05

There is __________ water.

06

some과 any 중에 빈칸에 들어갈 단어가 다른 하나를 고르세요.

① He doesn't drink ________ water.
② I bought ________ boxes.
③ ________ people liked him.
④ We have ________ plans for the future.

07

다음 중 밑줄 친 단어를 any로 바꿔야 하는 문장을 고르세요.

① Emily ate some cheese.
② I don't have some friends.
③ Would you like some candies?
④ Can I get some water?

08

다음 문장의 밑줄 친 부분을 바르게 고쳐 문장을 다시 쓰세요.

She can speak Italian, can she?

⇨ ____________________

09

다음 그림을 보고, 빈칸에 알맞은 수량 형용사를 [보기]에서 찾아 쓰세요.

[보기] many much a few a little

(1) __________ desks and chairs
(2) __________ students

10

다음 빈칸에 공통으로 들어갈 수 있는 말을 고르세요.

• I have __________ pencils.
• They bought __________ flour.

① much ② any ③ a lot of ④ a few

11

밑줄 친 부분이 틀린 문장을 고르세요.

① I have many cheese in my refrigerator.
② She didn't ask a lot of questions.
③ Would you like some tea?
④ Do you want to eat some bread?

12

다음 대화의 빈칸에 들어갈 부가의문문을 고르세요.

A: You should watch this movie.
B: Is it fun?
A: Yes. I watched it twice.
B: You really like the movie, __________

① don't you? ② do you?
③ are you? ④ aren't you?

13

다음 빈칸에 알맞은 부가의문문을 쓰세요.

(1) He doesn't know his uncle's name, __________

(2) We cleaned the room last night, __________

14

다음 빈칸에 공통으로 들어갈 알맞은 말을 고르세요.

(is / isn't)

A: He is a teacher, __________ he?
B: No, he __________. He's a doctor.

15

some과 any 중에서 빈칸에 공통으로 들어갈 알맞은 단어를 쓰세요.

• Can I get __________ coffee?
(제가 커피를 좀 얻을 수 있을까요?)
• I have __________ pictures in my room.
(나는 내 방에 사진 몇 점이 있다.)

[16~17] 부가의문문이 되도록 빈칸에 알맞은 말을 쓰세요.

16

It is so cold here, __________?

17

Paul loves her very much, __________?

[18~20] 다음 ( ) 안에서 알맞은 말에 ○표 하세요.

18

I need (a few / a little) sugar.

19

She bought (a few / a little) oranges.

20

Susan doesn't drink (many / much) juice.

21

다음 글을 읽고, 어색한 부분을 고르세요.

Dear diary,
It was really hot today. I couldn't open my eyes because of (A)a lot of sunshine. (B)A few classmates looked really tired. There were (C)little people on the street because of hot *weather.

* weather: 날씨

[22~23] ( ) 안에 주어진 말 중 알맞은 것을 고르세요.

22

Everyone (is / are) going to be happy.

23

All (student / students) (eat / eats) lunch at school.

24

다음 중 밑줄 친 부분이 틀린 것을 고르세요.

① She has few soap.
② I wrote some letters.
③ We spent little time together.
④ Mandy didn't know any Korean words.

25

다음 질문에 대한 대답으로 옳지 않은 것을 고르세요.

How many cups do you have?

① I have a few cups.
② I have few cups.
③ I have five cups.
④ I have a little cups.

[26~27] 빈칸에 공통으로 들어갈 말을 고르세요.

26

• Minsu ate ________ bread.
• Jiyoung bought ________ candies.

① a lot of ② many
③ few ④ much

27

• Sally isn't making ________ plans.
• Do you need ________ help?

① some ② any
③ much ④ many

28

부가의문문이 되도록 빈칸에 들어갈 말을 쓰세요.

A: I don't understand this story.
B: You didn't read it carefully, ________________?

29

다음 밑줄 친 부분이 틀린 문장을 고르세요.

① You work at the hospital, do you?
② He was in the kitchen, wasn't he?
③ She is not kind, is she?
④ We won't go to the zoo, will we?

30

다음 밑줄 친 부분이 틀린 문장을 고르세요.

① All the planes are in the air.
② Everyone have their free time.
③ All my friends are kind.
④ Every apple is fresh.

Chapter 03 There is / There are

이 챕터에서는 '~가 있다'의 의미를 갖는
'There is / There are' 표현을 배워 보아요.

☆ 학습 방향 및 배울 내용 미리보기 ☆

Unit 01 : **There is** a window.

There is / There are

There is와 There are 뒤에 각각 어떤 명사가 올 수 있는지 알아보아요.

▼

Unit 02 : There **was** a full moon.
Is there a book on the desk?

There is / There are의 과거 · 부정 · 의문형

There is와 There are의 과거형, 부정형, 의문형을 만드는 방법을 알아보아요.

단어 미리보기

이 챕터에 나올 단어들 중 이미 알고 있는 단어가 있나요?
맞는 뜻을 골라 체크해 봐요.

날짜 : 이름 : 알고 있는 단어의 수 : /24개

No.	아는 단어	단어	품사	알맞은 뜻에 체크 표시해 봐요.			
1	✔	honey	명사	꿀	✔	벌	☐
2	☐	full	형용사	빈	☐	가득한	☐
3	☐	broccoli	명사	브로콜리	☐	파	☐
4	☐	fresh	형용사	상한	☐	신선한	☐
5	☐	clock	명사	벽	☐	시계	☐
6	☐	enough	형용사	모자란	☐	충분한	☐
7	☐	tiger	명사	호랑이	☐	사자	☐
8	☐	duck	명사	오리	☐	닭	☐
9	☐	dolphin	명사	상어	☐	돌고래	☐
10	☐	giraffe	명사	기린	☐	얼룩말	☐
11	☐	table	명사	의자	☐	탁자	☐
12	☐	pencil case	명사	연필깎이	☐	필통	☐
13	☐	light	명사	빛	☐	그림자	☐
14	☐	end	명사	시작	☐	끝	☐
15	☐	chopstick	명사	숟가락	☐	젓가락	☐
16	☐	fall	명사	가을	☐	여름	☐
17	☐	dragonfly	명사	잠자리	☐	도마뱀	☐
18	☐	street	명사	가로수	☐	길	☐
19	☐	wind	명사	바람	☐	창문	☐
20	☐	way	명사	방법	☐	무게	☐
21	☐	lunch box	명사	공구함	☐	도시락	☐
22	☐	bottle	명사	병	☐	뚜껑	☐
23	☐	pencil	명사	연필	☐	지우개	☐
24	☐	star	명사	하늘	☐	별	☐

UNIT

01 There is a window.

There is/There are

'~가 있다'라고 말하고 싶을 때는 'There is / There are...' 표현을 사용해요.
원래 There는 '거기에'라는 뜻이지만 이 표현에서는 뜻이 없어져요.

❖ POiNT 1 ❖

There is + 셀 수 있는 명사의 단수형 / 셀 수 없는 명사

There is a window. 창문이 하나 있어.
There is an air conditioner. 에어컨이 한 대 있어.
There is a sofa. 소파가 하나 있어.
There is a girl. 여자 아이 한 명이 있어.
There is a dog. 개 한 마리가 있어.

셀 수 없는 명사는 아무리 양이 많아도 단수로 취급해요.

There is bread. 빵이 있어.
There is honey. 꿀이 있어.

❖ POiNT 2 ❖

There are + 셀 수 있는 명사의 복수형

There are many notebooks. 많은 공책들이 있어.
There are two pencil holders. 연필꽂이가 두 개 있어.
There are colored pencils. 색연필들이 있어.
There are paper clips. 종이 집게들이 있어.

Check and Write

다음 그림을 보고 ( ) 안에서 알맞은 것에 동그라미하고, 문장을 다시 쓰세요.

1. There (is / are) an apple. 사과가 한 개 있어.
   ➔ There is an apple.

2. There (is / are) much milk. 많은 우유가 있어.
   ➔ ______________________________.

3. There (is / are) three mushrooms. 버섯 세 개가 있어.
   ➔ ______________________________.

4. There (is / are) an empty cup. 빈 컵이 하나 있어.
   ➔ ______________________________.

5. There (is / are) fresh strawberries. 신선한 딸기들이 있어.
   ➔ ______________________________.

6. There (is / are) a head of broccoli. 브로콜리 한 송이가 있어.
   ➔ ______________________________.

정답과 해설 p.7

UNIT **02**

There is/There are의 과거 · 부정 · 의문형

There was a full moon. Is there a book on the desk?

❖ POiNT 1 ❖

There was/were '(과거에) ~이 있었다'

'(과거에) ~이 있었다'라고 말하고 싶을 땐 be동사를 과거형으로 바꿔주면 돼요.

There was a full moon.

보름달이 있었어.

There were lots of stars.

많은 별들이 있었어.

❖ POiNT 2 ❖

There is/are not '~이 없다'

'~이 없다'라고 말하고 싶을 땐 be동사 뒤에 not만 붙여주면 돼요.

There is not[isn't] a car.

차가 한 대도 없어.

There are not[aren't] any people.

사람이 하나도 없어.

❖ POiNT 3 ❖

Is/Are there~? '~이 있어?'

'~이 있어?'라고 말하고 싶을 땐 there와 be동사의 순서를 바꿔주면 돼요.

There + is a book on the desk.

책상 위에 책이 한 권 있어.

Is + there a book on the desk?

책상 위에 책이 한 권 있니?

*** 질문에 대한 대답은**

Yes, there is. (네, 있어요.) / No, there is not[isn't]. (아니요, 없어요.)

Check and Write

A 다음 그림을 보고 시점에 알맞게 문장을 완성하세요.

과거

현재

1. There ___were___ six students.
   여섯 명의 학생들이 있었다.
2. There __________ a teacher.
   선생님 한 분이 계셨다.
3. There __________ a book.
   책 한 권이 있었다.
4. There __________ a clock.
   시계 하나가 있다.
5. There __________ many desks.
   많은 책상들이 있다.
6. There __________ a black board.
   칠판 하나가 있다.

B 다음 (   ) 안에서 알맞은 것에 동그라미 하고, 문장을 다시 쓰세요.

1. There (is not / not is) enough time. 시간이 충분하지 않아.
   ➜ There is not enough time.
2. (There are not / Are there) any problems? 무슨 문제 있니?
   ➜ ____?
3. There (is / was) a small fight yesterday. 어제 작은 다툼이 있었어.
   ➜ ____.

CH 03

정답과 해설 p.7

Practice 1 문제를 풀면서 'There + be' 표현을 익혀 보아요.

우리말 뜻을 참고하여, 다음 빈칸에 들어갈 말로 적절한 것을 보기에서 골라 쓰세요. (중복 사용 가능)

A At the zoo

보기 is[Is] isn't are[Are] were[Were]

1. There ___are___ three tigers.
   세 마리의 호랑이들이 있어.

2. There ________ one big lion.
   한 마리의 큰 사자가 있어.

3. There ________ many ducks. 많은 오리들이 있어.

4. ________ there a lot of rabbits? 많은 토끼들이 있니?

5. There ________ a rabbit. 토끼가 한 마리도 없어.

6. ________ there many dolphins? 돌고래가 많이 있어?

7. There ________ not a dolphin. 돌고래가 한 마리도 없어.

8. ________ there monkeys in the tree?
   나무에 원숭이들이 있니?

9. There ________ a bird in the tree.
   나무에는 새 한 마리가 있어.

10. ________ there many giraffes at the zoo?
    동물원에 많은 기린들이 있었니?

정답과 해설 p.7

B In the house

보기	there[There]	is[Is]	are[Are]	isn't	aren't

1. There __________ a cat in the yard.
   마당에는 고양이 한 마리가 있어.

2. __________ are many windows in the house.
   그 집에는 많은 창문들이 있어.

3. There __________ a sofa in the living room.
   거실에는 소파 한 개가 있어.

4. __________ there bread on the table? 탁자 위에 빵이 있니?

5. No, there __________. 아니, 없어.

6. __________ there much milk in the bottle?
   병에 우유가 많니?

7. Yes, __________ __________.
   응, 많이 있어.

8. __________ there many dogs? 개들이 많이 있어?

9. No, __________ __________. 아니, 없어.

10. There __________ a hamster. 햄스터 한 마리가 있어.

정답과 해설 p.7

Practice 2 'There+be' 표현이 쓰인 문장을 완성해 보아요.

다음 우리말 뜻과 같도록 주어진 표현을 순서에 맞게 배열하여 문장을 완성하세요.

1. (a girl, is, There).

여자 아이 한 명이 있어.

➔ There is a girl ______________________.

2. (are, There, two children).

두 명의 어린이들이 있어.

➔ ______________________ ______________________.

3. (friends, are, There, many) around you. 네 주위에는 많은 친구들이 있어.

➔ ______________________ around you.

4. (Are, dogs, there) in your home? 너희 집에 개들이 있니?

➔ ______________________ in your home?

5. Yes, (are, there). 응, 있어.

➔ Yes, ______________________.

6. (three dogs, are, There) in the yard.

마당에는 세 마리의 개가 있어.

➔ ______________________ in the yard.

정답과 해설 p.7

7. (there, Are, cats) in your home? 너희 집에 고양이들이 있니?

➔ ______________________ in your home?

8. No, (not, are, there). 아니, 없어.

➔ No, ______________________.

9. (is, There, delicious food) on the table.

탁자 위에 맛있는 음식이 있어.

➔ ______________________ on the table.

10. (There, a child, was not) in the playground.

놀이터에는 아이가 한 명도 없었어.

➔ ______________________ in the playground.

11. (were, There, many students) in the classroom.

교실에는 많은 학생들이 있었어.

➔ ______________________ in the classroom.

12. (are, There, things, a lot of) in the living room.

거실에는 많은 것들이 있어.

➔ ______________________ in the living room.

13. (a student, There, is not) here. 이곳에는 학생이 한 명도 없어.

➔ ______________________ here.

CH 03

정답과 해설 p.7

14. (juice, is, There) in the bottle. (*bottle: 병)
병에는 주스가 있어.

➔ ______________________________ in the bottle.

15. (were not, any books, There) in my bag. 내 가방에 책들이 하나도 없었어.

➔ ______________________________ in my bag.

16. (there, Is, a pencil case) in your bag?
네 가방에 필통이 있니?

➔ ______________________________
in your bag?

17. (many problems, were, There).
많은 문제들이 있었어.

➔ ______________________________
______________________________.

18. (at the end of the tunnel, There is, light).
터널의 끝에 빛이 있어.

➔ ______________________________
______________________________.

19. (any problem, Is, there)? 무슨 문제라도 있어?

➔ ______________________________?

20. No, (is, not, there). 아니, 없어.

➔ No, ______________________________.

정답과 해설 p.7

Practice 3 'There+be' 표현을 써서 완전한 문장을 써 보아요.

우리말 뜻을 참고하여 주어진 표현을 사용해 문장을 영어로 완성하세요.

1. (a tree)

마당에 나무 한 그루가 있었어.

→ There was a tree ____________
in the yard.

2. (a cat)

길 위에 고양이 한 마리가 있어.

→ ____________
on the street.

3. (any chopsticks) 젓가락 있니?

→ ____________________________?

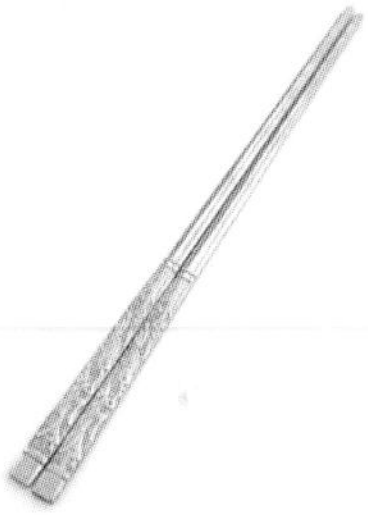

4. (a tree) 지금은 여기에 나무 한 그루도 없어.

→ ____________________________ here now.

5. (many dragonflies) (*dragonfly: 잠자리)

가을에는 많은 잠자리들이 있어.

→ ____________________________ in the fall.

6. (dragonflies) 겨울에 잠자리가 있니?

→ ____________________________ in the winter?

정답과 해설 p.7

7. (a mother cat) 길 위에 어미 고양이가 있니?

➔ ______________________________ on the street?

8. (there) 아니, 없어.

➔ No, ______________________________.

9. (many comic books)

만화책이 많이 없었어.

➔ ______________________________

______________________________.

10. (a piece of cake)

케이크 한 조각이 있어.

➔ ______________________________

______________________________.

11. (any time for a nap) (*nap: 낮잠)

낮잠을 잘 시간이 없었어.

➔ ______________________________.

12. (a shortcut) (*shortcut: 지름길)

지름길은 하나도 없어.

➔ ______________________________.

13. (any chopsticks) 도시락에 젓가락이 없었어.

➔ ______________________________ in the lunch boxes.

정답과 해설 p.7

14. (many video games) 비디오 게임이 많이 있니?

➔ ____?

15. (a way) (*way: 방법)

방법이 없었어.

➔ ____.

16. (four potatoes) 감자 네 개가 있어.

➔ ____.

17. (any wind)

어제 바람 한 점 없었어.

➔ ____________________ yesterday.

18. (a subway station)

당신의 집 근처에 지하철역이 하나 있나요?

➔ ____________________ near your house?

19. (a chocolate bar) 초코바 한 개가 있어.

➔ ____.

20. (many ways) 방법은 많아.

➔ ____.

정답과 해설 p.8

Let's Practice More!

SET 01

학습목표 1 | 'there'의 쓰임을 구분할 수 있어요.　　공부한 날 :　　맞은 개수 :　　/12개

다음 밑줄 친 부분이 '거기에, 그곳에서'라고 해석되면 ○, 따로 해석되지 않으면 ×표 하세요.

01. There is a window in the house. → ×

02. Mina met him there. → ______

03. There is a cat in the yard. → ______

04. There is a girl. → ______

05. I want to go there. → ______

06. There was a post office. → ______

07. What time is it now over there? → ______

08. He is still there. → ______

09. Are there a lot of rabbits? → ______

10. Is she living there? → ______

11. I was there to find him. → ______

12. There is a piece of cake. → ______

정답과 해설 p.8

Let's Practice More!

SET 02

학습목표 2 | 'There + be' 표현의 쓰임을 익혀 보아요. 공부한 날 : 맞은 개수 : /14개

다음 ( ) 안에서 알맞은 것에 동그라미 하세요.

01. There (is / are) bread. 빵이 있다.

02. There (is / are) one big lion. 큰 사자 한 마리가 있어.

03. (Is / Are) there dogs in your home? 너의 집에는 개들이 있니?

04. There (was / were) many students in the classroom.
교실에는 많은 학생들이 있었어.

05. There (is / are) a cat on the street. 길 위에 고양이 한 마리가 있어.

06. There (was / were) not any time for a nap. 낮잠을 잘 시간이 없었어.

07. There (is / are) many ducks. 많은 오리들이 있어.

08. There (is / are) two children. 두 명의 어린이들이 있어.

09. There (is / are) delicious food on the table. 탁자 위에 맛있는 음식이 있어.

10. There (is / are) not a student here. 이곳에는 학생이 한 명도 없어.

11. (Is / Are) there any problem? 무슨 문제라도 있어?

12. There (is / are) many ways. 방법은 많아.

13. (Is / Are) there many video games? 비디오 게임이 많이 있니?

14. There (is / are) many dragonflies in the fall.
가을에는 많은 잠자리들이 있어.

정답과 해설 p.8

Let's Practice More!

SET 03

학습목표 2 | 'There + be' 표현의 쓰임을 익혀 보아요. 공부한 날 : 맞은 개수 : /14개

우리말 뜻과 같은 뜻이 되도록 There is(was)/There are(were) 중 알맞은 것을 골라 쓰세요.

01. There is bread. 빵이 있다.

02. ________ a lot of things in the living room. 거실에는 많은 것들이 있어.

03. ________ juice in the bottle. 병에는 주스가 있어.

04. ________ not any books in my bag. 내 가방에 책들이 하나도 없었어.

05. ________ light at the end of the tunnel. 터널의 끝에 빛이 있어.

06. ________ not a shortcut. 지름길은 하나도 없어.

07. ________ not any wind yesterday. 어제 바람 한 점 없었어.

08. ________ four potatoes. 감자 네 개가 있어.

09. ________ a bird in the tree. 나무에는 새 한 마리가 있어.

10. ________ many friends around you. 네 주위에는 많은 친구들이 있어.

11. ________ three dogs in the yard. 마당에는 세 마리의 개가 있어.

12. ________ not a child in the playground. 놀이터에는 아이가 한 명도 없었어.

13. ________ many problems. 많은 문제들이 있었어.

14. ________ a chocolate bar. 초코바 한 개가 있어.

정답과 해설 p.8

Let's Practice More!

SET 04

학습목표 2 | 'There + be' 표현의 쓰임을 익혀 보아요. 공부한 날 : 맞은 개수 : /14개

다음 밑줄 친 부분을 알맞게 고치세요.

01. There is many notebooks. 많은 공책들이 있다. → are

02. There are not a dolphin. 돌고래가 한 마리도 없어. → ______

03. Was there many giraffe(s) at the zoo? 동물원에 많은 기린들이 있었니? → ______

04. There is two children. 두 명의 어린이들이 있어. → ______

05. Are there a mother cat on the street? 길 위에 어미 고양이가 있니? → ______

06. There were not a way. 방법이 하나도 없었어. → ______

07. Is there monkeys in the tree? 나무에 원숭이들이 있니? → ______

08. Are there any problem? 무슨 문제라도 있어? → ______

09. No, there is not cats. 아니, 고양이들이 없어. → ______

10. There are not any student here. 이곳에는 학생이 한 명도 없어. → ______

11. There are a desk in my room. 내 방에는 책상이 한 개 있다. → ______

12. Is there dogs in your home? 너희 집에 개들이 있니? → ______

13. Is there any chopsticks? 젓가락 있니? → ______

14. There was not many comic books. 만화책이 많지 않았어. → ______

정답과 해설 p.8

Let's Practice More!

SET 05

학습목표 3 | 'There + be' 표현의 과거형과 현재형을 비교해 보아요. 공부한 날 : 맞은 개수 : /12개

다음 밑줄 친 부분의 해석으로 알맞은 것에 동그라미 하세요.

01. There was a full moon. → (있다 / 있었다)

02. There is a car. → (있다 / 있었다)

03. There was a tree in the yard. → (있다 / 있었다)

04. There are two potatoes. → (있다 / 있었다)

05. There are many ways. → (있다 / 있었다)

06. There were many problems. → (있다 / 있었다)

07. There are many dragonflies in the fall. → (있다 / 있었다)

08. There is milk in the bottle. → (있다 / 있었다)

09. There are many ducks. → (있다 / 있었다)

10. There was a child in the playground. → (있다 / 있었다)

11. There was an accident yesterday. → (있다 / 있었다)

12. There is a chocolate bar. → (있다 / 있었다)

정답과 해설 p.8

Let's Practice More!

SET 06

학습목표 4 | 'There+be' 표현의 부정문을 알아보아요. 공부한 날 : 맞은 개수 : /14개

다음 ( ) 안에서 알맞은 것에 동그라미 하세요.

01. There (does not / is not) much milk in the bottle.
병에 우유가 많이 있지 않아.

02. There (is not / not is) light at the end of the tunnel.
터널의 끝에 빛이 없어.

03. There (is not / not is) a piece of cake. 케이크가 한 조각도 없어.

04. There (not was / was not) any time for a nap. 낮잠을 잘 시간이 없었어.

05. There (are not / not are) many ways. 방법이 많지 않아.

06. There (is not / are not) a pencil case in your bag. 네 가방에 필통이 없어.

07. There (not was / was not) a child in the playground.
놀이터에는 아이가 한 명도 없었어.

08. There (don't / are not) cats in your home.
너희 집에 고양이들이 없어.

09. There (didn't / were not) many dolphins.
돌고래가 많지 않았어.

10. There (is not / not is) a hamster. 햄스터가 하나도 없어.

11. No, there (are not / not are) cats. 아니, 고양이들이 없어.

12. There (is not / not is) a book. 책이 하나도 없다.

13. There (not were / were not) many students in the classroom.
교실에는 학생들이 많이 있지 않았어.

14. There (is not / not is) a shortcut. 지름길은 하나도 없어.

정답과 해설 p.8

Let's Practice More!

SET 07

학습목표 5 | 'There+be' 표현의 의문문을 알아보아요.　　공부한 날 :　　맞은 개수 :　　/20개

다음 평서문을 의문문으로 바꿔 쓰세요.

01.

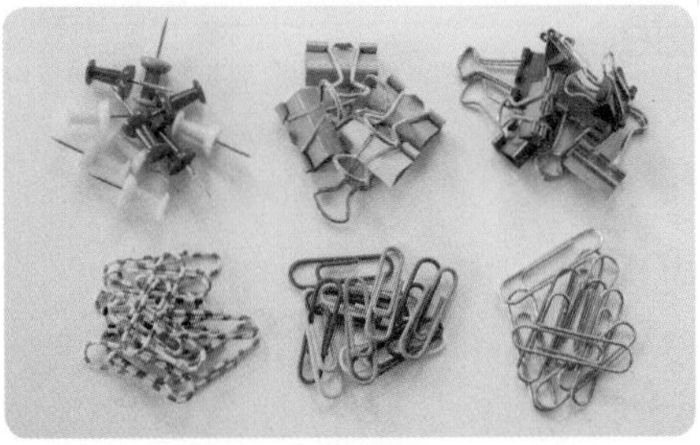

There are paper clips.

종이 집게들이 있다.

➔ Are there paper clips ?

02.

There was a tree.

나무 한 그루가 있었어.

➔ ____________________?

03. There are many video games. 비디오 게임이 많아.

➔ ____________________?

04. There is a dog on the street. 길 위에 개 한 마리가 있어.

➔ ____________________?

05. There are five carrots. 당근 다섯 개가 있어.

➔ ____________________?

06. There were many novels. 소설이 많았어.

➔ ____________________?

07. There was a way. 방법이 하나 있었어.

➔ ____________________?

08. There were many problems. 많은 문제들이 있었어.

➔ ____________________?

09. There is delicious food on the table.

탁자 위에 맛있는 음식이 있어.

➔ ____________________?

정답과 해설 p.8

10. There is a monkey in the tree. 나무에 원숭이가 한 마리 있어.

➔ ____?

11. 

There was a strong wind.
강한 바람이 있었어(불었어).

➔ ____________________?

12. 

There is a chocolate bar.
초코바 한 개가 있어.

➔ ____________________?

13. There were many giraffe(s) at the zoo. 동물원에 많은 기린들이 있었어.

➔ ____?

14. There is a sofa in the living room. 거실에는 소파가 한 개 있어.

➔ ____?

15. There is much Coke in the bottle. 병에 콜라가 많다.

➔ ____?

16. There are two children. 두 명의 어린이들이 있어.

➔ ____?

17. There are many friends around you. 네 주위에는 많은 친구들이 있어.

➔ ____?

18. There are three dogs in the yard. 마당에는 세 마리의 개가 있어.

➔ ____?

19. There is bread on the table. 탁자 위에 빵이 있어.

➔ ______________________________________?

20. There is one big lion. 큰 사자 한 마리가 있어.

➔ ____?

정답과 해설 p.8

Let's Practice More!

SET 08

학습목표 5 | "There+be' 표현의 의문문을 알아보아요. 공부한 날 : 맞은 개수 : /20개

다음 질문에 대한 알맞은 답변이 될 수 있도록 ( ) 안에서 알맞은 것을 고르세요.

01. Q: Is there a subway station near your house? 너희 집 근처에 지하철역이 하나 있니?
A: No, (there isn't / there not is). 아니, 없어.

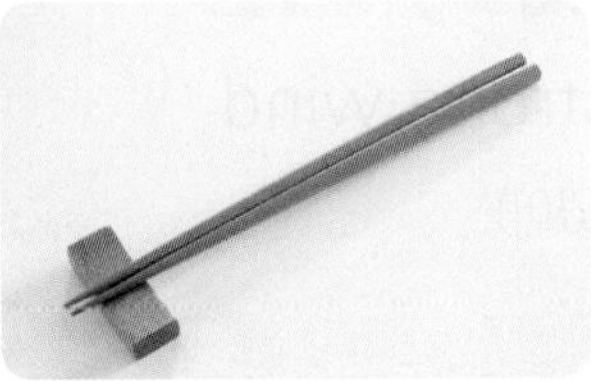

02. Q: Are there any chopsticks? 젓가락 있니?
A: Yes, (there are / are there). 응, 있어.

03. Q: Are there many video games? 비디오 게임이 많이 있니?
A: No, (there not are / there aren't). 아니, 없어.

04. Q: Are there dragonflies in the winter? 겨울에 잠자리가 있니?
A: No, (there aren't / there not are). 아니, 없어.

05. Q: Is there a mother cat on the street? 길 위에 어미 고양이 한 마리가 있니?
A: Yes, (there is / is there). 응, 있어.

06. Q: Is there any problem? 무슨 문제라도 있어?
A: No, (there isn't / there is). 아니, 없어.

07. Q: Is there a pencil case in your bag? 네 가방에 필통이 있니?
A: Yes, (there isn't / there is). 응, 있어.

08. Q: Are there a lot of rabbits? 많은 토끼들이 있니?
A: Yes, (there are / there is). 응, 있어.

09. Q: Are there monkeys in the tree? 나무에 원숭이들이 있니?
A: No, (there isn't / there aren't). 아니, 없어.

10. Q: Is there much milk in the bottle? 병에 우유가 많니?
A: No, (there isn't / there not is). 아니, 없어.

정답과 해설 p.8

11. Q: Is there bread on the table? 탁자 위에 빵이 있니?
A: Yes, (there isn't / there is). 응, 있어.

12. Q: Are there many dogs in the park? 공원에 개들이 많이 있어?
A: Yes, (there are / there is). 응, 있어.

13. Q: Are there cats in your home? 너희 집에 고양이들이 있니?
A: No, (there not are / there aren't). 아니, 없어.

14. Q: Was there a child in the playground? 놀이터에 아이가 한 명 있었니?
A: No, (there wasn't / there weren't). 아니, 없었어.

15. Q: Is there a cow in the yard? 마당에 소 한 마리가 있니?
A: Yes, (there not is / there is). 응, 있어.

16. Q: Was there a tree in the yard? 마당에 나무 한 그루가 있었니?
A: Yes, (there were / there was). 응, 있었어.

17. Q: Is there a glass of water? 물 한 잔이 있니?
A: No, (there isn't / there not is). 아니, 없어.

18. Q: Are there three sweet potatoes? 고구마 세 개가 있니?
A: Yes, (there is / there are). 응, 있어.

19. Q: Were there any books in your bag? 네 가방에 책들이 있었니?
A: No, (there were / there weren't). 아니, 없었어.

20. Q: Is there a shortcut? 지름길이 하나 있니?
A: No, (there isn't / there not is). 아니, 없어.

정답과 해설 p.8

Chapter 04 비교급 / 최상급

이 챕터에서는 둘 또는 그 이상의 대상의 성질이나 상태를 비교할 때 쓰는 비교급,
그리고 대상들 중 '가장 ~한 것'을 표현하는 최상급에 대해 배워 보아요.

☆ 학습 방향 및 배울 내용 미리보기 ☆

☐ **Unit 01 :** The giraffe is **taller than** me.

비교급 (1)

비교급을 만드는 네 가지 규칙 중 두 가지 규칙을 먼저 알아보아요.

▼

☐ **Unit 02 :** The elephant is **bigger than** the mouse.

비교급 (2)

비교급을 만드는 나머지 두 가지 규칙과 불규칙적인 비교급에 대해 알아보아요.

▼

☐ **Unit 03 :** This is **the cheapest** smart phone.

최상급 (1)

최상급을 만드는 네 가지 규칙 중 두 가지 규칙을 먼저 알아보아요.

▼

☐ **Unit 04 :** It is **the most interesting** book.

최상급 (2)

최상급을 만드는 나머지 두 가지 규칙과 불규칙적인 최상급에 대해 알아보아요.

단어 미리보기

이 챕터에 나올 단어들 중 이미 알고 있는 단어가 있나요?
맞는 뜻을 골라 체크해 봐요.

날짜 : 이름 : 알고 있는 단어의 수 : /24개

No.	아는 단어	단어	품사	알맞은 뜻에 체크 표시해 봐요.			
1	✔	turtle	명사	거북이	✔	토끼	☐
2	☐	cheap	형용사	비싼	☐	싼	☐
3	☐	warm	형용사	따뜻한	☐	차가운	☐
4	☐	mouse	명사	고양이	☐	쥐	☐
5	☐	low	형용사	낮은	☐	높은	☐
6	☐	famous	형용사	인기 없는	☐	유명한	☐
7	☐	quickly	부사	빠르게	☐	느리게	☐
8	☐	when	접속사	~할 때	☐	왜냐하면	☐
9	☐	noisy	형용사	조용한	☐	시끄러운	☐
10	☐	taxi	명사	버스	☐	택시	☐
11	☐	high	형용사	높은	☐	낮은	☐
12	☐	pen	명사	칼	☐	펜	☐
13	☐	blood	명사	피	☐	눈물	☐
14	☐	wide	형용사	넓은	☐	좁은	☐
15	☐	black	형용사	검은	☐	파란	☐
16	☐	pork	명사	소고기	☐	돼지고기	☐
17	☐	surprising	형용사	놀라운	☐	즐거운	☐
18	☐	store	명사	가게	☐	집	☐
19	☐	actor	명사	행동	☐	배우	☐
20	☐	world	명사	세계	☐	벽	☐
21	☐	popular	형용사	인기 있는	☐	가난한	☐
22	☐	mountain	명사	강	☐	산	☐
23	☐	score	명사	점수	☐	중심	☐
24	☐	subject	명사	인기	☐	과목	☐

UNIT

01 The giraffe is taller than me.

비교급 (1)

❖ POiNT 1 ❖

비교급의 개념

The giraffe is tall. 기린은 (키가) 크다.

I am short. 나는 (키가) 작다.

tall과 short는 각각 '기린'과 '나'의 성질을 나타내죠?
만약, '기린은 나보다 더 크다'나 '나는 기린보다 더 작다'라고 표현하고 싶다면 어떻게 해야 할까요?
형용사나 부사를 이용해서 둘 또는 그 이상의 대상의 성질이나 상태를 비교할 때 쓰는 게 바로 비교급이에요.

The giraffe is taller than me. 기린은 나보다 (키가) 더 크다.

I am shorter than the giraffe. 나는 기린보다 (키가) 더 작다.

'(키가) 큰'이라는 뜻을 가진 tall의 비교급 'taller'는 '(키가) 더 큰'이라는 뜻을 가져요.
여기에 '~보다'라는 뜻을 가지는 'than'을 붙여주면 비교급이 완성돼요!

❖ POiNT 2 ❖

비교급 만들기 – 규칙적 비교급 비교급 형태를 만드는 네 가지 규칙 중 두 가지를 먼저 알려줄게요.

1. 형용사 · 부사의 기본형 + –er (단, e로 끝나는 단어들은 + –r)

This pencil is longer than that one. (형용사 long의 비교급)
이 연필은 저것보다 더 길다.

I studied harder than Mina. (부사 hard의 비교급)
나는 미나보다 더 열심히 공부했어.

A rabbit runs faster than a turtle. (부사 fast의 비교급)
토끼는 거북이보다 더 빨리 달린다.

2. 형용사 · 부사의 기본형이 y로 끝날 경우 y를 i로 고치고 + –er

She is heavier than me. (형용사 heavy의 비교급)
그녀는 나보다 더 무거워.

I got up earlier than mom. (부사 early의 비교급)
나는 엄마보다 더 일찍 일어났어.

Check and Write

A 다음 단어를 비교급 형태로 바꿔보세요.

1. strong → stronger 더 강한

2. late → ________ 더 늦은, 더 늦게

3. healthy → ________ 더 건강한

4. cheap → ________ 더 싼

5. busy → ________ 더 바쁜

CH 04

B 주어진 단어를 비교급으로 고쳐 빈칸을 채워보세요.

1. old 나이가 많은
   → My father is older than my mother. 나의 아버지는 어머니보다 나이가 더 많으시다.

2. fast 빨리
   → A cheetah runs ____________ a snail. 치타는 달팽이보다 더 빨리 달린다.

정답과 해설 p.9

비교급 (2)

UNIT 02 The elephant is bigger than the mouse.

❖ POiNT 1 ❖

앞에서 비교급 형태를 만드는 두 가지 규칙을 배웠죠? 나머지 두 가지 규칙은 아래와 같아요.

3. 형용사 · 부사의 기본형이 「단모음 + 단자음」으로 끝나는 경우 ⇨ 마지막 자음 한번 더 쓰고 + –er

*단모음은 모음 앞·뒤로 자음이 오는 것을, 단자음은 자음 앞·뒤로 모음이 오는 것을 뜻해요.

bigger than
~보다 큰

hotter than
~보다 뜨거운

fatter than
~보다 뚱뚱한

4. ① 대부분의 2음절 이상의 형용사(–y로 끝나는 형용사 제외) ② 분사형태의 형용사
③ 「형용사 + ly」 형태의 부사의 경우 ⇨ more + 형용사 · 부사의 기본형

*음절은 끊어 읽는 발음의 수예요. 예를 들면 beautiful은 beau·ti·ful(뷰/티/풀)로 3음절이에요.

more famous than
~보다 더 유명한

more tired than
~보다 더 피곤한

more quickly than
~보다 더 빠르게

❖ POiNT 2 ❖

불규칙적 비교급 비교급 형태를 만드는 네 가지 규칙에 어긋나는 단어들도 있어요.

good/well 좋은 / 좋게 ⇨ better than ~보다 좋은 / ~보다 좋게

bad 나쁜 ⇨ worse than ~보다 나쁜

many/much 많은 ⇨ more than ~보다 많은

little 적은 ⇨ less than ~보다 적은

Check and Write

A 다음 단어를 비교급 형태로 바꿔보세요.

1. sad → sadder 더 슬픈

2. happily → ______ 더 행복하게

3. much → ______ 더 많은

4. beautiful → ______ 더 아름다운

5. good → ______ 더 좋은

B 비교급 형태로 알맞은 단어에 동그라미하고, 문장을 다시 쓰세요.

1. A lion is (biger / bigger) than a mouse.

→ A lion is bigger than a mouse.

사자는 쥐보다 더 커.

2. He speaks (more quietly / quietlier) than others.

→ ______________________________.

그는 다른 사람들보다 더 작게 말해.

정답과 해설 p.9

Practice 1 문제를 풀면서 비교급을 익혀 보아요.

우리말 해석을 참고하여 보기 에서 알맞은 단어를 골라 비교급으로 변형하여 빈칸에 써 보세요.

A Seoul vs. Busan

보기 low cold soon warm beautiful

1. I will arrive in Busan ____sooner____ than 5 o'clock.
나는 부산에 5시보다 더 일찍 도착할거야.

2. Seoul is ____________ than Busan.
서울은 부산보다 추워.

3. Busan is ____________ than Seoul. 부산은 서울보다 따뜻해.

4. Rents in Busan are ____________ than in Seoul. (*rents: 집세)
부산에서의 집세가 서울보다 더 낮아.

5. I think Busan is ____________ than Seoul.
나는 부산이 서울보다 더 아름답다고 생각해.

B Boni vs. Hani

보기 well tall famous early

1. Hani is ____________ than Boni. 하니는 보니보다 유명해.

2. Boni is ____________ than Hani. 보니는 하니보다 키가 커.

3. Hani dances ____________ than Boni does.
하니는 보니보다 춤을 잘 춰.

4. Boni arrives at the studio ____________ than Hani does.
보니는 하니보다 촬영장에 일찍 도착해.

정답과 해설 p.9

C Rabbit vs. Turtle

보기	young	long	soon	slow	fast	old

1. The rabbit is ____________________ than the turtle.
   그 토끼는 그 거북이보다 나이가 적어.

2. The turtle is ____________________ than the rabbit.
   그 거북이는 그 토끼보다 나이가 많아.

3. A turtle lives ____________________ than a rabbit. 거북이는 토끼보다 오래 살아.

4. A rabbit runs ____________________ than a turtle.
   토끼는 거북이보다 빨리 달려.

5. A turtle is ____________________ than a rabbit.
   거북이는 토끼보다 느려.

6. The turtle arrives ____________________ than the rabbit.
   그 거북이는 그 토끼보다 더 일찍 도착해.

D Book vs. Movie vs. Game

보기	much	interesting	exciting	quickly	happy

1. My older sister read the book ____________________ than me.
   언니는 나보다 책을 더 빨리 읽었어.

2. She looks ____________________ than me when we read the book.
   우리가 책을 읽을 때 그녀는 나보다 더 행복해 보여.

3. I like movies ____________________ than books.
   나는 책보다 영화가 더 좋아.

4. A movie is ________________________________ than a book.
   영화는 책보다 흥미로워.

5. But a game is ________________________________ than a movie.
   하지만 영화보다 게임이 더 재미있어.

정답과 해설 p.9

Practice 2 비교급 표현을 써서 문장을 완성해 보아요.

다음 우리말 뜻과 같도록 주어진 표현을 순서에 맞게 배열하여 문장을 완성하세요.

1. (faster, than a bus, An airplane is). 비행기는 버스보다 빨라.

➔ An airplane is faster than a bus.

2. (than a taxi, noisier, A bus is). 버스는 택시보다 시끄러워.

➔ ______________________________.

3. (than a taxi, expensive, An airplane is, more). 비행기는 택시보다 더 비싸.

➔ ______________________________.

4. (more, The train was, comfortable than) I expected. (*comfortable: 편한)
기차는 내가 기대했던 것보다 더 편했어.

➔ ______________________________ I expected.

5. (than a car, more dangerous, A motorcycle is). 오토바이가 자동차보다 더 위험해.

➔ ______________________________.

6. (sweeter, vegetables, Fruits are, than).
과일은 채소보다 더 달아.

➔ ______________________________.

7. (heavier than, A watermelon is, a melon). 수박은 메론보다 더 무거워.

➔ ______________________________.

8. (sourer than, Lemons are, oranges). (*sour: 신)
레몬은 오렌지보다 더 셔.

➔ ______________________________.

9. (than meat, healthier, Vegetables are) for your health.
채소가 고기보다 너의 건강에 더 좋아.

➔ ______________________________ for your health.

10. (friendship, more important than, Nothing is).
우정보다 중요한 것은 없어.

➔ ______________________________.

정답과 해설 p.9

11. *Pooh* : (braver, You are, than you believe).
푸우 : 너는 네가 믿는 것보다 더 용감해.

➜ ____.

12. (than I do, earlier, My mother gets up). 엄마는 나보다 더 일찍 일어나셔.

➜ ____.

13. (earlier than me, was born, My twin sister).
내 쌍둥이 언니는 나보다 일찍 태어났어.

➜ ______________________________________.

14. (taller than, She was, me). 그녀가 나보다 키가 컸었어.

➜ ____.

15. (me, prettier than, Is she)? 그녀가 나보다 예뻐?

➜ ____?

16. (thicker than, Blood is, water). 피는 물보다 진하다. **(*thick: 진한)**

➜ ____.

17. (mightier than, The pen is, the sword). **(*mighty: 강한)**
펜은 칼보다 강하다.

➜ ______________________________________.

18. (than words, Actions speak, louder).
행동은 말보다 큰 소리를 낸다. (행동이 말보다 더 중요하다.)

➜ ____.

19. (better than, Two heads are, one). 하나보다는 둘이 더 낫다. (백지장도 맞들면 낫다.)

➜ ____.

20. (better than, A good neighbor is, a distant cousin).
좋은 이웃이 먼 친척보다 낫다. **(*neighbor: 이웃, distant: 먼, cousin: 친척)**

➜ ____.

정답과 해설 p.9

Practice 3 비교급 표현을 써서 완전한 문장을 써 보아요.

다음 주어진 단어를 비교급으로 고쳐 빈칸을 알맞게 채워보세요.

1. (much) 나는 공부하는 것보다 쇼핑하는 게 더 좋아.
   ➔ I like shopping ___more___ than studying.

2. (cheap) 이 노트가 저것보다 더 싸.
   ➔ This notebook is ______________ than that one.

3. (pretty) 남색 바지가 하얀색 바지보다 더 예뻐.
   ➔ Navy pants are ______________ than white pants.

4. (small) 이 셔츠는 내가 생각했던 것보다 작아.
   ➔ This shirt is ______________ than I thought.

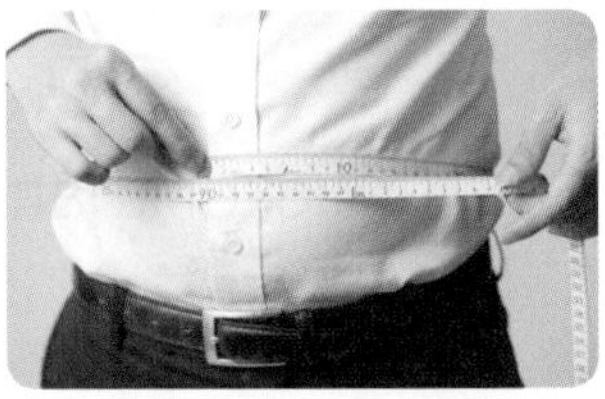

5. (fat) 나는 작년보다 올해 더 뚱뚱해.
   ➔ I am ______________ this year than last year.

6. (interesting) 영어는 수학보다 더 흥미로워.
   ➔ English is ________________________ than math.

7. (difficult) 수학은 영어보다 더 어려워.
   ➔ Math is ______________ than English.

8. (hard) 나는 어제보다 오늘 영어를 더 열심히 공부했어.
   ➔ I studied English ______________ today than yesterday.

9. (high) 나는 영어시험에서 준우보다 더 높은 성적을 받았어.
   ➔ I got a ______________ mark than Junwoo on the English exam.

10. (well) 나는 엄마보다 영어 말하기를 더 잘해.
    ➔ I speak English ______________ than mom does.

정답과 해설 p.9

11. (quickly) (*adult: 어른)
아이들은 어른보다 더 빨리 영어를 배워.

➔ Children learn English ______________________ than adults.

12. (small) 그 아기는 그의 형보다 더 작아.

➔ The baby is ______________ than his brother.

13. (slowly) 그녀는 그녀의 아기보다 더 천천히 걸어.

➔ She walks ______________ than her baby.

14. (late) 나는 전보다 더 늦게 잤다.

➔ I slept ______________ than before.

15. (early) 하지만 나는 어제보다 더 일찍 일어났어.

➔ But I got up ______________ than yesterday.

16. (tired) 그래서 나는 어제보다 더 피곤해.

➔ So I am ____________________ than yesterday.

17. (strong) 아이언맨이 스파이더맨보다 강해.

➔ Iron Man is ______________ than Spider Man.

18. (old) 그는 그의 형보다 나이가 더 많아 보인다.

➔ He looks ______________ than his brother.

19. (much) 그는 그의 형보다 더 많이 먹어.

➔ He eats ______________ than his brother.

20. (dirty) (*public restroom: 공중화장실)
휴대전화는 공중화장실보다 더 더러울 수도 있다.

➔ A cell phone can be ______________ than a public restroom.

CH 04

정답과 해설 p.9

Let's Practice More!

SET 01

학습목표 1 | 형용사와 부사의 올바른 비교급 형태를 알아보아요. 공부한 날 : 맞은 개수 : /12개

다음 빈칸에 형용사나 부사의 비교급을 쓰세요.

01. tall
(키가) 큰
→ taller

02. smart
똑똑한
→ ____________

03. large
큰
→ ____________

04. cold
추운
→ ____________

05. strong
강한
→ ____________

06. late
늦은, 늦게
→ ____________

07. fast
빠른, 빨리
→ ____________

08. long
긴
→ ____________

09. hard
어려운, 단단한, 열심히
→ ____________

10. cheap
(값이) 싼
→ ____________

11. kind
친절한
→ ____________

12. old
(나이가) 많은
→ ____________

정답과 해설 p.9

Let's Practice More!

SET 02

학습목표 1 | 형용사와 부사의 올바른 비교급 형태를 알아보아요.　　공부한 날 :　　맞은 개수 :　　/14개

다음 빈칸에 형용사나 부사의 비교급을 쓰세요.

01. dirty 더러운 → dirtier

02. noisy 시끄러운 → ______

03. fat 뚱뚱한 → ______

04. heavy 무거운 → ______

05. healthy 건강한 → ______

06. big 큰 → ______

07. funny 웃기는 → ______

08. pretty 예쁜 → ______

09. mighty 강한, (힘이) 센 → ______

10. sad 슬픈 → ______

11. hot 뜨거운 → ______

12. lazy 게으른 → ______

13. happy 행복한 → ______

14. early 이른, 일찍 → ______

정답과 해설 p.9

Let's Practice More!

SET 03

학습목표 1 | **형용사와 부사의 올바른 비교급 형태를 알아보아요.** 공부한 날 : 맞은 개수 : /14개

다음 빈칸에 형용사나 부사의 비교급을 쓰세요.

01. interesting 흥미로운 → more interesting

02. exciting 신나는 → ____________

03. easily 쉽게 → ____________

04. slowly 느리게 → ____________

05. dangerous 위험한 → ____________

06. important 중요한 → ____________

07. quickly 빠르게 → ____________

08. beautiful 아름다운 → ____________

09. famous 유명한 → ____________

10. expensive 비싼 → ____________

11. heavily 심하게 → ____________

12. tired 피곤한 → ____________

13. happily 행복하게 → ____________

14. difficult 어려운 → ____________

정답과 해설 p.9

Let's Practice More!

SET 04

학습목표 1 | 형용사와 부사의 올바른 비교급 형태를 알아보아요. 공부한 날 : 맞은 개수 : /12개

다음 빈칸에 형용사나 부사의 비교급을 쓰세요.

01. good
좋은
→ better

02. little
(양이) 적은
→ ____________________

03. soon
곧
→ ____________________

04. many
(수가) 많은
→ ____________________

05. warm
따뜻한
→ ____________________

06. bad
나쁜
→ ____________________

07. slow
느린
→ ____________________

08. well
잘
→ ____________________

09. dry
마른
→ ____________________

10. much
(양이) 많은
→ ____________________

11. low
낮은
→ ____________________

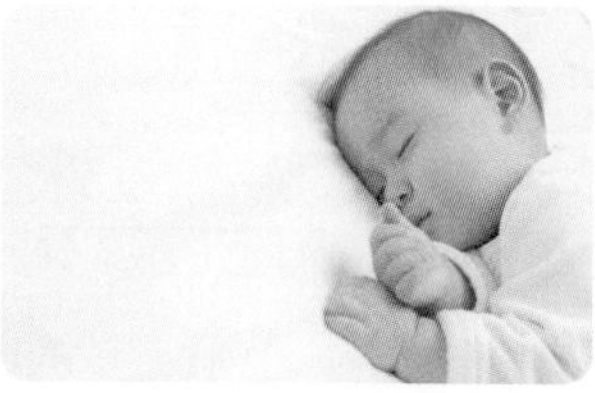

12. young
어린
→ ____________________

정답과 해설 p.9

Let's Practice More!

SET 05

학습목표 2 | 비교급 문장을 공부해 보아요.　　공부한 날 :　　맞은 개수 :　　/14개

우리말 해석과 일치하도록 다음 밑줄 친 부분을 알맞게 고쳐보세요.

01. A cheetah is fast than a snail. → faster
치타는 달팽이보다 빨라.

02. Seoul is cold than Busan. → ____
서울은 부산보다 추워.

03. Boni is tall than Hani. → ____
보니는 하니보다 키가 커.

04. An airplane is expensive than a taxi. → ____
비행기는 택시보다 더 비싸.

05. A bus is noisy than a taxi. → ____
버스는 택시보다 시끄러워.

06. A turtle lives long than a rabbit. → ____
거북이는 토끼보다 오래 살아.

07. The train was comfortable than I expected. → ____
기차는 내가 기대했던 것보다 더 편했어.

08. Vegetables are healthy than meat for your health. → ____
채소가 고기보다 너의 건강에 더 좋아.

09. Is she pretty than me? → ____
그녀가 나보다 예뻐?

10. Actions speak loud than words. → ____
행동은 말보다 큰 소리를 낸다. (행동이 말보다 더 중요하다.)

11. Two heads are good than one. → ____
하나보단 둘이 더 낫다. (백지장도 맞들면 낫다.)

12. Blood is thick than water. → ____
피는 물보다 진하다.

13. This notebook is cheap than that one. → ____
이 노트가 저것보다 더 싸.

14. I like shopping much than studying. → ____
나는 공부하는 것보다 쇼핑하는 게 더 좋아.

정답과 해설 p.9

Let's Practice More!

SET 06

학습목표 2 | 비교급 문장을 공부해 보아요. 공부한 날 : 맞은 개수 : /14개

다음 ( ) 안의 단어를 활용하여 비교급 문장을 만들어 보세요.

01. The giraffe is ______taller______ than me. (tall)
기린은 나보다 키가 커.

02. My mother is ____________ than my father. (old)
나의 어머니는 나의 아버지보다 나이가 많으셔.

03. She walks ____________ than her baby. (slowly)
그녀는 그녀의 아기보다 더 천천히 걸어.

04. He eats ____________ than his brother. (much)
그는 그의 형보다 더 많이 먹어.

05. I got up ____________ than yesterday. (early)
나는 어제보다 더 일찍 일어났어.

06. I slept ____________ than before. (late)
나는 전보다 더 늦게 잤다.

07. I will arrive in Busan ____________ than 5 o'clock. (soon)
나는 부산에 5시보다 더 일찍 도착할거야.

08. Rents in Busan are ____________ than in Seoul. (low)
부산에서의 집세가 서울보다 더 낮아.

09. The rabbit is ____________ than the turtle. (young)
그 토끼는 그 거북이보다 나이가 어려.

10. My older sister read the book ____________ than me. (quickly)
나의 언니는 나보다 책을 더 빨리 읽었어.

11. I like movies ____________ than books. (much)
나는 책보다 영화가 더 좋아.

12. A game is ____________ than a movie. (exciting)
영화보다 게임이 더 재미있어.

13. A motorcycle is ____________ than a car. (dangerous)
오토바이가 자동차보다 더 위험해.

14. Nothing is ____________ than friendship. (important)
우정보다 중요한 것은 없어.

정답과 해설 p.10

Let's Practice More!

SET 07

학습목표 2 | 비교급 문장을 공부해 보아요. 공부한 날 : 맞은 개수 : /20개

다음 문장에서 밑줄 친 부분이 맞으면 ○를, 틀리면 바르게 고쳐 보세요.

01.

The baby is smaller by his brother.
그 아기는 그의 형보다 더 작아.
➔ than his brother

02.

She was taller from me.
그녀는 나보다 키가 컸었어.
➔ ______________

03. This shirt is smaller than that one. ➔ ______________
이 셔츠는 저것보다 작아.

04. Navy pants are more pretty than white pants. ➔ ______________
남색 바지가 하얀색 바지보다 더 예뻐.

05. I am more fat this year than last year. ➔ ______________
나는 작년보다 올해 더 뚱뚱해.

06. English is more interesting than math. ➔ ______________
영어는 수학보다 더 흥미로워.

07. Math is more difficult to English. ➔ ______________
수학은 영어보다 더 어려워.

08. I studied English harder than math. ➔ ______________
나는 수학보다 영어를 더 열심히 공부했어.

09. I speak English more well than my mom does. ➔ ______________
나는 나의 엄마보다 영어 말하기를 더 잘해.

10. Children learn English quicklier than adults. ➔ ______________
아이들은 어른보다 더 빨리 영어를 배워.

정답과 해설 p.10

11. He looks older than his brother. ➔ ______________

그는 그의 형보다 나이가 더 많아 보인다.

12. Lemons are sourer than oranges. ➔ ______________

레몬은 오렌지보다 더 셔.

13.

A watermelon is heavier than a melon.

수박은 메론보다 더 무거워.

➔ ______________

14.

Fruits are sweetier than vegetables.

과일은 채소보다 더 달아.

➔ ______________

15. You are more brave than you believe. ➔ ______________

너는 네가 믿는 것보다 더 용감해.

16. My mother gets up earlier than I do. ➔ ______________

나의 엄마는 나보다 더 일찍 일어나셔.

17. My twin sister was born earlier than me. (*be born: 태어나다) ➔ ______________

내 쌍둥이 언니는 나보다 일찍 태어났어.

18. A good neighbor is good than a distant cousin. ➔ ______________

좋은 이웃이 먼 친척보다 낫다.

19. A cell phone can be dirtier than a public restroom. ➔ ______________

휴대전화는 공중화장실보다 더 더러울 수도 있어.

20. Iron Man is strongger than Spider Man. ➔ ______________

아이언맨이 스파이더맨보다 강해.

정답과 해설 p.10

Let's Practice More!

SET 08

학습목표 2 | 비교급 문장을 공부해 보아요.　　공부한 날 :　　맞은 개수 :　　/20개

다음 문장이 우리말 해석과 같은 뜻이 되도록 (　) 안의 단어를 활용하여 빈칸을 채워보세요.

01.

A rabbit runs ___faster than___ a turtle. (fast)

토끼는 거북이보다 빨리 달려.

02.

Apples are ______________ tomatoes. (sweet)

사과는 토마토보다 더 달아.

03. I think Busan is ______________ Seoul. (beautiful)

나는 부산이 서울보다 더 아름답다고 생각해.

04. Hani is ______________ Boni. (famous)

하니는 보니보다 유명해.

05. Hani dances ______________ Boni does. (well)

하니는 보니보다 춤을 잘 춰.

06. Boni arrives at the studio ______________ Hani does. (early)

보니는 하니보다 촬영장에 일찍 도착해.

07. Busan is ______________ Seoul. (warm)

부산은 서울보다 따뜻해.

08. The turtle is ______________ the rabbit. (old)

그 거북이는 그 토끼보다 나이가 많아.

09. The turtle arrives ______________ the rabbit. (soon)

그 거북이는 그 토끼보다 더 일찍 도착해.

정답과 해설 p.10

10. She looks ______________ me. (happy)
그녀는 나보다 더 행복해 보여.

11. An airplane is ______________ a bus. (fast)
비행기는 버스보다 빨라.

12. 

The chair is ______________ than I expected. (comfortable)
의자는 내가 기대했던 것보다 더 편해.

13. 

My mother is ______________ my father. (old)
나의 어머니는 아버지보다 나이가 더 많으셔.

14. My dad sleeps ______________ me. (late)
나의 아빠는 나보다 더 늦게 주무셔.

15. I eat ______________ my brother. (much)
나는 나의 오빠보다 많이 먹어.

16. He is ______________ his mom. (heavy)
그는 그의 엄마보다 더 무거워.

17. The pen is ______________ the sword. (mighty)
펜은 칼보다 강하다.

18. She speaks ______________ us. (slowly)
그녀는 우리보다 더 천천히 말해.

19. Actions speak ______________ words. (loud)
행동은 말보다 큰 소리를 낸다. (행동이 말보다 더 중요하다.)

20. A lion is ______________ a mouse. (big)
사자는 쥐보다 더 커.

정답과 해설 p.10

UNIT 최상급 (1)

03 This is the cheapest smart phone.

❖ POiNT 1 ❖

최상급 만들기

최상급은 비교 대상이 되는 것들 중 성질이나 상태의 정도가 '가장 ~한 것'을 표현해요.

This is the cheapest smart phone.
이것은 가장 싼 스마트폰이야.

형용사나 부사를 최상급 형태로 바꿔 주고 그 앞에 the를 붙여요.
단, 부사의 경우 the를 생략할 수 있어요.

❖ POiNT 2 ❖

규칙적 최상급

최상급 형태를 만드는 네 가지 규칙 중 두 가지를 먼저 알아보아요.

1. 형용사 · 부사의 기본형 + -est (단, e로 끝나는 단어들은 + -st)

the oldest
가장 늙은

the longest
가장 긴

the latest
가장 최신의

2. 형용사 · 부사의 기본형이 y로 끝날 경우 y를 i로 고치고 + -est

the funniest
가장 웃기는

the easiest
가장 쉬운

the heaviest
가장 무거운

Check and Write

A 다음 형용사를 최상급 형태로 바꿔보세요.

1. tall → the tallest 가장 키가 큰

2. wide → the ______ 가장 폭이 넓은

3. happy → the ______ 가장 행복한

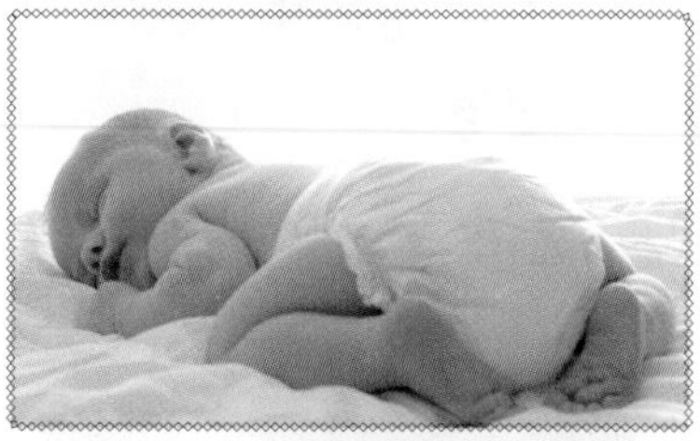

4. young → the ______ 가장 어린

5. lucky → the ______ 가장 운이 좋은

B 다음 우리말 뜻과 일치하도록 ( ) 안에서 알맞은 것에 동그라미 하세요.

1. Lion is the (stronger / strongest) animal.
   사자는 가장 강한 동물이야.

2. She is the (smart / smartest) student in this class.
   그녀는 이 반에서 가장 똑똑한 학생이야.

정답과 해설 p.10

UNIT

04 It is the most interesting book.

최상급 (2)

❖ POiNT 1 ❖

앞에서 최상급 만드는 두 가지 규칙을 배웠죠? 나머지 두 가지 규칙을 마저 익혀 보아요.

3. 형용사 · 부사의 기본형이 「단모음 + 단자음」으로 끝나는 경우 ⇨ 마지막 자음 한 번 더 쓰고 + -est

the biggest
가장 큰

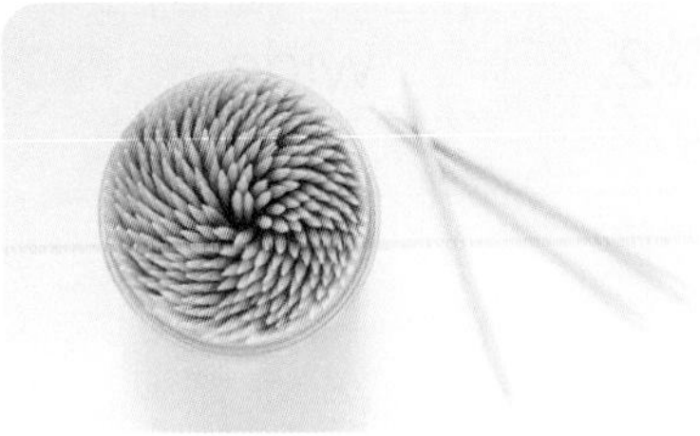
the thinnest
가장 가는

the saddest
가장 슬픈

4. ① 대부분의 2음절 이상의 형용사(-y로 끝나는 형용사 제외) ② 분사형태의 형용사
③ 「형용사 + ly」 형태의 부사의 경우 ⇨ the most + 형용사 · 부사의 기본형

*음절은 끊어 읽는 발음의 수예요. 예를 들면 beautiful은 beau·ti·ful(뷰/티/풀)로 3음절이에요.

the most dangerous
가장 위험한

the most interesting
가장 재미있는

the most slowly
가장 느리게

❖ POiNT 2 ❖

불규칙적 최상급 네 가지 규칙에 어긋나는 단어들도 있어요.

- good/well 좋은/좋게 ⇨ the best 가장 좋은/가장 좋게
- bad 나쁜 ⇨ the worst 가장 나쁜/최악의
- many/much 많은 ⇨ the most 가장 많은
- little 적은 ⇨ the least 가장 적은

Check and Write

A **다음 형용사를 최상급 형태로 바꿔보세요.**

1. hot → the hottest
가장 더운

2. difficult → the ____________
가장 어려운

3. surprising → the ____________
가장 놀라운

4. fat → the ____________
가장 뚱뚱한

5. bad → the ____________
가장 나쁜, 최악의

B **다음 우리말 뜻과 일치하도록 ( ) 안에서 알맞은 것에 동그라미 하세요.**

1. He became the (famousest / most famous) singer.
그는 가장 유명한 가수가 되었어.

2. It was the (hotest / hottest) day.
가장 더운 날이었어.

3. I got the (goodest / best) score on the test.
나는 시험에서 최고 점수를 받았어.

정답과 해설 p.10

Practice 1 문제를 풀면서 최상급 표현을 익혀 보아요.

보기 에서 알맞은 단어를 골라 최상급으로 변형하여 빈칸에 써 보세요.

A The kingdom of animals

보기	fast	tall	big	old	smart	fat

1. This is the ___fastest___ lion. 이건 가장 빠른 사자야.
2. That is the __________ camel. 저건 가장 큰 낙타야. (*camel: 낙타)
3. The giraffe is the __________ animal.
   기린은 가장 키가 큰 동물이야. (*giraffe: 기린)

4. I saw the __________ pig. 나는 가장 뚱뚱한 돼지를 봤어.
5. We have the __________ parrot. (*parrot: 앵무새)
   우리는 가장 똑똑한 앵무새를 갖고 있어.
6. You can see the __________ turtle at the zoo.
   넌 동물원에서 가장 나이 많은 거북이를 볼 수 있어.

B Special times in our life

보기	cold	busy	exciting	meaningful	short

1. It was the __________ year of my life. (*meaningful: 의미 있는)
   (올해는) 내 삶에서 가장 의미 있는 해였어.
2. January is the __________ month of the year.
   1월은 한 해 중 가장 추운 달이야.
3. Last week was the __________ week of the month.
   지난 주는 한 달 중 가장 바쁜 주였어.
4. Yesterday was the __________ day of the week.
   어제는 한 주 중 가장 짧은 날이었어.
5. Lunch time is the __________ time of the day.
   점심시간은 하루 중 가장 신나는 시간이야.

정답과 해설 p.10

C Hello, Jeju!

보기 high big delicious beautiful

1. Jeju Island is the ______________ island in Korea.
제주도는 한국에서 가장 아름다운 섬이야.

2. It is also the ______________ island in Korea.
그곳은 또한 한국에서 가장 큰 섬이야.

3. Hallasan is the ______________ mountain on Jeju Island.
한라산은 제주도에서 가장 높은 산이야.

4. Grilled black pork is the ______________ food on Jeju Island.
흑돼지 구이는 제주도에서 가장 맛있는 음식이야.

D Amusement park (*amusement park: 놀이공원)

보기 popular exciting boring fast long

1. The roller coaster is the ______________ ride at the amusement park. 롤러코스터는 그 놀이공원에서 가장 빠른 놀이기구야. (*ride: 놀이기구)

2. Is it the ______________ roller coaster in Korea?
그거 한국에서 가장 긴 롤러코스터야?

3. The ______________ ride is the merry-go-round. (*merry-go-round: 회전목마)
가장 지루한 놀이기구는 회전목마야.

4. The Viking is the ______________ to me.
나한텐 바이킹이 제일 짜릿해.

5. And it is the ______________ ride.
그리고 그건 가장 인기 있는 놀이기구야.

정답과 해설 p.10

Practice 2 최상급 표현을 써서 문장을 완성해 보아요.

다음 우리말 뜻과 같도록 주어진 표현을 순서에 맞게 배열하여 문장을 완성하세요.

1. (difficult, question, the most, It is).
그건 가장 어려운 질문이야.

→ It is the most difficult question.

2. (votes, the most, You got).
(*vote: 표, 투표하다)
너는 가장 많은 표를 받았어.

→ ______________________.

3. (not, I'm, the smartest, student) in our class.
내가 우리 반에서 가장 똑똑한 학생은 아니야.

→ ______________________ in our class.

4. (student, the most, diligent, I am) in the class. (*diligent: 성실한)
난 우리 반에서 가장 성실한 학생이야.

→ ______________________ in the class.

5. (Today is, day, the greatest) of my life!
오늘은 제 인생에서 가장 멋진 날이에요!

→ ______________________ of my life!

6. (restaurant, It is, the most, popular) in this city.
그곳은 이 도시에서 가장 인기 있는 음식점이야.

→ ______________________ in this city.

정답과 해설 p.10

7. (What is, food, the most, delicious) at this restaurant?
이 식당에서 가장 맛있는 음식이 뭐예요?

➔ ______________________________ at this restaurant?

8. (The steak is, expensive item, the most) on the menu.
스테이크가 메뉴에서 가장 비싼 품목이야.

➔ ______________________________

__________ on the menu.

9. (fearful person, Mom is, the most) I know. (*fearful: 무서운)
엄마는 내가 아는 가장 무서운 사람이야.

➔ ______________________________

__________ I know.

10. (the most, English is, difficult subject)! (*subject: 과목)
영어는 가장 어려운 과목이야!

➔ ______________________________!

11. (I will order, dish, the cheapest) on the menu. (*order: 주문하다)
나는 메뉴에서 가장 싼 요리를 주문할래.

➔ ______________________________ on the menu.

12. (the hardest, is always, The first step). 첫 걸음은 항상 가장 어렵다.

➔ ______________________________.

13. (may have, potential, You, the greatest) of all. (*potential: 가능성)
너에게 가장 큰 가능성이 있을지도 몰라.

➔ ______________________________ of all.

정답과 해설 p.10

14. (the most, What are, important traits) in a friend? (*trait: 특징)
친구에게 있어서 가장 중요한 특징이 무엇이니?

➔ ______________________________ in a friend?

15. (the luckiest, Charlie was, boy) around.
Charlie는 주위에서 가장 운 좋은 소년이었어.

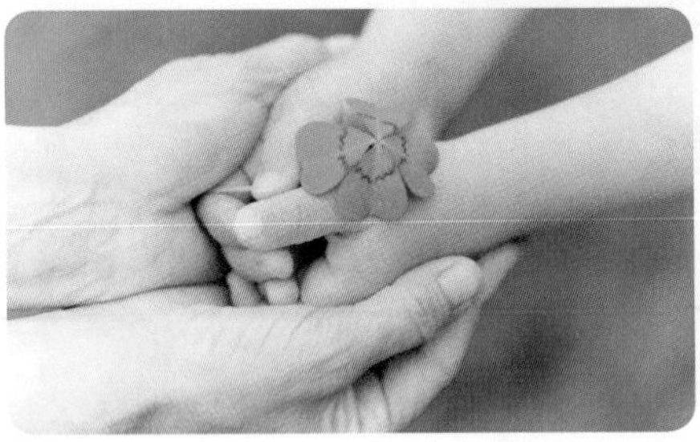

➔ ______________________________
______________ around.

16. (the most, has, She, beautiful voice).
그녀는 가장 아름다운 목소리를 가지고 있어.

➔ ______________________________
______________________________.

17. (the worst, It was, choice) of my life. 그건 내 생애 최악의 선택이었어.

➔ ______________________________ of my life.

18. (of them, the shortest, She is). 그녀는 그들 중 키가 제일 작아.

➔ ______________________________.

19. (the highest, Mount Everest is, mountain) in the world.
에베레스트 산은 세계에서 가장 높은 산이야.

➔ ______________________________ in the world.

20. (the best, Honesty, is, policy). (*policy: 정책, 방책)
정직이 최선의 방책이다.

➔ ______________________________.

정답과 해설 p.10

Practice 3 최상급 표현을 써서 완전한 문장을 써 보아요.

다음 주어진 표현을 사용하여 우리말 뜻에 맞게 문장을 완성해 보세요.
(단, 제시된 형용사는 최상급으로 바꿔쓰세요.)

1. (My little brother, cute)

내 남동생은 세상에서 제일 귀여워!

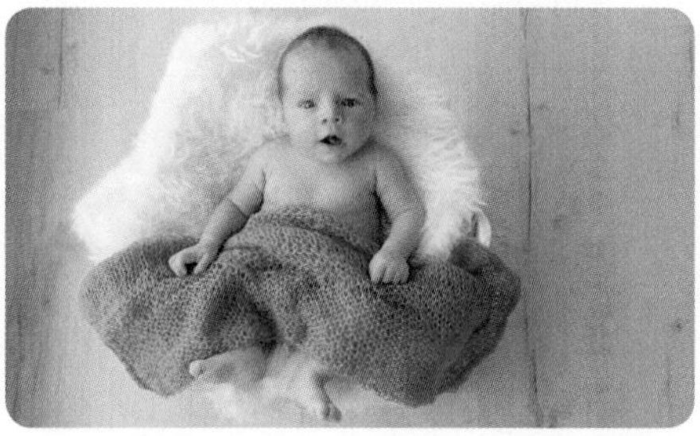

→ My little brother is the cutest

in the world!

2. (smart, girl)

그녀는 우리 학교에서 가장 똑똑한 여자아이야.

→ ______________________

in my school.

3. (It, famous, song) 그건 역대 가장 유명한 노래야.

→ ______________________ of all time.

4. (kind, boy) 그는 우리 팀에서 가장 친절한 남자아이야.

→ ______________________ on my team.

5. (noisy, kid) 그는 그 방에서 가장 시끄러운 아이야.

→ ______________________ in the room.

6. (pretty, girl) 가장 예쁜 여자아이가 그곳에 살았어요.

→ ______________________ lived there.

정답과 해설 p.10

7. (My grandfather, old)

나의 할아버지는 우리 가족 중에서 제일 나이가 많으셔.

➔ ______________________ in my family.

8. (expensive, chocolate)

그녀는 가장 비싼 초콜릿을 선택했어.

➔ She chose __________

______________________.

9. (young)

나는 우리 가족 중에서 제일 어려.

➔ I am ______________

in my family.

10. (interesting, play) (*play: 연극)

이건 가장 재밌는 연극이야!

➔ This is ______________________________!

11. (handsome, actor) (*actor: 배우)

저 남자는 무대에서 가장 잘생긴 배우야.

➔ That man is ______________________________ on stage.

12. (bad, movie) 이건 최악의 영화야!

➔ This is ______________________________!

13. (beautiful, figure skater)

나는 김연아가 세계에서 가장 아름다운 피겨 스케이트 선수라고 생각해.

➔ I think Yuna Kim is ______________________ in the world.

정답과 해설 p.10

14. (high, score) 그녀는 올림픽에서 가장 높은 점수를 얻었어.

➜ She got ______________________________ at the Olympics.

15. (fast, train) 저건 한국에서 제일 빠른 기차야.

➜ That is ________________________ in Korea.

16. (happy, moment) (*moment: 순간)

그건 내 인생에서 가장 행복한 순간이었어.

➜ It was ____________

____________ of my life.

17. (nice, sister)

나는 가장 멋진 누나가 될 거야.

➜ I will be ____________

____________ of all.

18. (cheap, t-shirt) 이것이 그 상점에서 가장 싼 티셔츠야.

➜ __________________________________ in the store.

19. (always, do their best) (*do one's best: 최선을 다하다)

그들은 항상 최선을 다해.

➜ ____.

20. (good) 이 컴퓨터는 가게 안에서 가장 좋아.

➜ This computer is ___________________________ in the store.

정답과 해설 p.10

Let's Practice More!

SET 01

학습목표 1 | **형용사와 부사의 올바른 최상급 형태를 알아보아요.** 공부한 날 : 맞은 개수 : /12개

다음 빈칸에 주어진 단어의 최상급을 쓰세요.

01. old 나이가 든 → the oldest

02. hard 어려운, 단단한, 열심히 → ____________

03. cheap (가격이) 싼 → ____________

04. long (길이가) 긴 → ____________

05. high 높은, 높이 → ____________

06. tall 키가 큰 → ____________

07. short 키가 작은 → ____________

08. great 훌륭한 → ____________

09. strong 강한 → ____________

10. smart 똑똑한 → ____________

11. young 어린 → ____________

12. cold 차가운 → ____________

정답과 해설 p.10

Let's Practice More!

SET 02

학습목표 1 | 형용사와 부사의 올바른 최상급 형태를 알아보아요. 공부한 날 : 맞은 개수 : /14개

다음 빈칸에 주어진 단어의 최상급을 쓰세요.

01. funny 웃기는 → the funniest

02. easy 쉬운 → ______

03. big 큰 → ______

04. hot 뜨거운 → ______

05. fat 뚱뚱한 → ______

06. sad 슬픈 → ______

07. pretty 예쁜 → ______

08. lucky 운이 좋은 → ______

09. happy 행복한 → ______

10. heavy 무거운 → ______

11. busy 바쁜 → ______

12. noisy 시끄러운 → ______

13. lazy 게으른 → ______

14. dirty 더러운 → ______

정답과 해설 p.11

CH 04

Let's Practice More!

SET 03

학습목표 1 | 형용사와 부사의 올바른 최상급 형태를 알아보아요. 공부한 날 : 맞은 개수 : /14개

다음 빈칸에 주어진 단어의 최상급을 쓰세요.

01. dangerous 위험한 → the most dangerous

02. important 중요한 → ____________

03. popular 인기 많은 → ____________

04. boring 시무한 → ____________

05. delicious 맛있는 → ____________

06. diligent 성실한 → ____________

07. difficult 어려운 → ____________

08. exciting 신나는 → ____________

09. fearful 무서운 → ____________

10. meaningful 의미 있는 → ____________

11. expensive (값이) 비싼 → ____________

12. interesting 재미있는 → ____________

13. beautiful 아름다운 → ____________

14. handsome 잘생긴 → ____________

정답과 해설 p.11

Let's Practice More!

SET 04

학습목표 1 | 형용사와 부사의 올바른 최상급 형태를 알아보아요.　공부한 날 :　맞은 개수 : /12개

다음 빈칸에 주어진 단어의 최상급을 쓰세요.

01. good 좋은 → the best

02. bad 나쁜 → ______

03. slowly 느리게  → ______

04. wide 넓은 → ______

05. well 잘, 좋게 → ______

06. nice 좋은, 즐거운 → ______

07. many (수가) 많은 → ______

08. late 늦은  → ______

09. much (양이) 많은 → ______

10. famous 유명한 → ______

11. little (양이) 적은 → ______

12. surprising 놀라운 → ______

정답과 해설 p.11

Let's Practice More!

SET 05

학습목표 2 | 최상급 문장을 공부해 보아요. 공부한 날 : 맞은 개수 : /14개

다음 ( ) 안에서 알맞은 최상급 형태를 골라보세요.

01. This is the (faster / fastest) lion. 이건 가장 빠른 사자야.

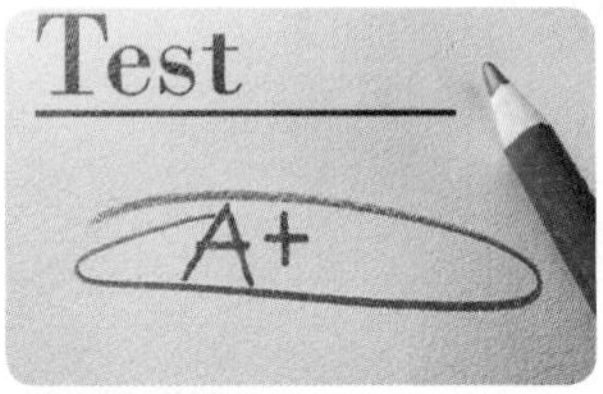

02. I got the (goodest / best) score on the test.
나는 그 시험에서 가장 좋은 점수를 받았어.

03. Last week was the (busyest / busiest) week of the month.
지난 주는 한 달 중 가장 바쁜 주였어.

04. It is the (popularest / most popular) ride. 그건 가장 인기 있는 놀이기구야.

05. It is the (bigest / biggest) island in Korea. 그곳은 한국에서 가장 큰 섬이야.

06. The (boringest / most boring) ride is the merry-go-round.
가장 지루한 놀이기구는 회전목마야.

07. Charlie was the (luckiest / luckyest) boy around.
Charlie는 주위에서 가장 운 좋은 소년이었어.

08. It was the (badest / worst) choice of my life.
그건 내 생애 최악의 선택이었어.

09. The (prettiest / prettyest) girl lived there. 가장 예쁜 여자아이가 그곳에 살았어.

10. I will be the (niceest / nicest) sister of all. 나는 가장 멋진 누나가 될 거야.

11. I am the (young / youngest) in my family.
나는 우리 가족 중에서 제일 어려.

12. It was the (happiest / happyest) moment of my life.
그건 내 인생에서 가장 행복한 순간이었어.

13. She chose the (expensivest / most expensive) chocolate.
그녀는 가장 비싼 초콜릿을 선택했어.

14. This is the (worst / baddest) movie! 이건 최악의 영화야!

정답과 해설 p.11

Let's Practice More!

SET 06

학습목표 2 | 최상급 문장을 공부해 보아요. 공부한 날 : 맞은 개수 : /14개

( ) 안의 단어를 사용하여 최상급 문장을 완성하세요.

01. Today is __the coldest__ day of the year. (cold)
오늘은 올해 중 가장 추운 날이야.

02. That is ______________ camel. (big) 저건 가장 큰 낙타야.

03. We have ______________ parrot. (smart) 우리는 가장 똑똑한 앵무새를 갖고 있어.

04. You can see ______________ turtle at the zoo. (old)
넌 동물원에서 가장 나이 많은 거북이를 볼 수 있어.

05. Grilled black pork is ______________ food on Jeju Island. (delicious)
흑돼지 구이는 제주도에서 가장 맛있는 음식이야.

06. The roller coaster is ______________ ride at the amusement park. (fast)
롤러코스터는 그 놀이공원에서 가장 빠른 놀이기구야.

07. It was ______________ year of my life. (meaningful)
(올해는) 내 삶에서 가장 의미 있는 해였어.

08. I'm not ______________ student in our class. (smart)
내가 우리 반에서 가장 똑똑한 학생은 아니야.

09. The first step is always ______________. (hard) 첫 걸음은 항상 가장 어렵다.

10. What are ______________ traits in a friend? (important)
친구에게 있어서 가장 중요한 특징이 무엇이니?

11. It was ______________ choice of my life. (bad) 그건 내 생애 최악의 선택이었어.

12. Mount Everest is ______________ mountain in the world. (high)
에베레스트 산은 세계에서 가장 높은 산이야.

13. Honesty is ______________ policy. (good)
정직이 최선의 방책이다.

14. Mom is ______________ person I know. (fearful)
엄마는 내가 아는 가장 무서운 사람이야.

정답과 해설 p.11

Let's Practice More!

SET 07

학습목표 2 | 최상급 문장을 공부해 보아요. 공부한 날 : 맞은 개수 : /20개

다음 최상급 문장의 밑줄 친 부분을 바르게 고쳐 쓰세요.

01. 

The cheetah is the faster animal.
치타는 가장 빠른 동물이야.

→ fastest

02. 

The giraffe is the tall animal.
기린은 가장 키가 큰 동물이야.

→ ______________

03. This is the more interesting play! → ______________
이건 가장 재밌는 연극이야!

04. She got the higher score at the Olympics. → ______________
그녀는 올림픽에서 가장 높은 점수를 받았어.

05. My grandfather is the old in my family. → ______________
나의 할아버지는 우리 가족 중에서 제일 나이가 많으셔.

06. I saw the fatter pig. → ______________
나는 가장 뚱뚱한 돼지를 봤어.

07. Jeju Island is the beautifulest island in Korea. → ______________
제주도는 한국에서 가장 아름다운 섬이야.

08. She is the shorter of them. → ______________
그녀는 그들 중 키가 제일 작아.

09. I will order the most cheap dish. → ______________
나는 가장 싼 요리를 주문할래.

10. He is the kindeest boy on my team. → ______________
그는 우리 팀에서 가장 친절한 남자아이야.

정답과 해설 p.11

11. 

The Viking is the more exciting to me.
나한텐 바이킹이 제일 짜릿해.

→ ______________

12. 

We have the more smarter dog.
우리는 가장 똑똑한 개를 가지고 있어.

→ ______________

13. He is the noisyest kid in the room. → ______________
그는 그 방에서 가장 시끄러운 아이야.

14. What is the deliciousest food at this restaurant? → ______________
이 식당에서 가장 맛있는 음식이 뭐예요?

15. I think Yuna Kim is the more beautiful figure skater in the world. → ______________
나는 김연아가 세계에서 가장 아름다운 피겨 스케이트 선수라고 생각해.

16. That is the faster train in Korea. → ______________
저건 한국에서 제일 빠른 기차야.

17. Hallasan is the high mountain on Jeju Island. → ______________
한라산은 제주도에서 가장 높은 산이야.

18. Yesterday was the shorttest day of the week. → ______________
어제는 한 주 중 가장 짧은 날이었어.

19. January is the colder month of the year. → ______________
1월은 한 해 중 가장 추운 달이야.

20. You got the many votes. → ______________
너는 가장 많은 표를 받았어.

정답과 해설 p.11

Let's Practice More!

SET 08

학습목표 3 | 최상급과 비교급을 구분해 보아요. 공부한 날 : 맞은 개수 : /20개

다음 문장이 우리말 뜻과 같도록 ( ) 안의 단어를 활용하여 빈칸을 채워 보세요.

01.

My little brother is ___the cutest___ in the world! (cute)

내 남동생은 세상에서 제일 귀여워!

02.

She is __________ student in this class. (tall)

그녀는 이 반에서 가장 키가 큰 학생이다.

03. She has __________ voice. (beautiful)

그녀는 가장 아름다운 목소리를 가지고 있어.

04. English is __________ than math. (difficult)

영어는 수학보다 어려워.

05. The steak is __________ than the pasta. (expensive)

스테이크가 파스타보다 더 비싸.

06. My father is __________ than my mother. (old)

나의 아버지는 나의 어머니보다 나이가 많으셔.

07. This computer is __________ in the store. (good)

이 컴퓨터는 가게 안에서 가장 좋아.

08. Mina is __________ than me. (lucky)

미나는 나보다 운이 좋아.

09. Math is __________ than English. (interesting)

수학은 영어보다 더 흥미로워.

정답과 해설 p.11

10. 

I became ____________________
than last year. (fat)
나는 작년보다 더 뚱뚱해졌어.

11. 

English is ____________________
subject! (difficult)
영어는 가장 어려운 과목이야!

CH 04

12. Today is ____________________ day of my life! (great)
오늘은 제 인생에서 가장 멋진 날이에요!

13. A good neighbor is ____________________ than a distant cousin. (good)
좋은 이웃이 먼 친척보다 낫다.

14. The rabbit is ____________________ than the turtle. (young)
그 토끼는 그 거북이보다 나이가 적어.

15. It was ____________________ moment of her life. (happy)
그건 그녀의 인생에서 가장 행복한 순간이었어.

16. Honesty is ____________________ policy. (good)
정직이 최선의 방책이다.

17. He is ____________________ student in his class. (diligent)
그는 그의 반에서 가장 성실한 학생이야.

18. A giraffe is ____________________ than a lion. (tall)
기린은 사자보다 키가 커.

19. You may have ____________________ potential of all. (great)
너에게 가장 큰 가능성이 있을지도 몰라.

20. A watermelon is ____________________ than a melon. (heavy)
수박은 멜론보다 더 무거워.

정답과 해설 p.11

실전테스트

CHAPTER 03~04

공부한 날 :
복습한 날 :
부모님 확인 :

CHAPTER 03 There is/There are　CHAPTER 04 비교급/최상급

● 정답과 해설은 별책 11쪽에서 확인하세요!!

01

다음 그림을 보고, 일치하지 않는 문장을 고르세요.

① Birds are under the tree.
② There is a tree in the picture.
③ There are two people in the picture.
④ They are standing in front of the tree.

02

그림을 잘못 묘사한 문장을 고르세요.

① There are two people in the picture.
② The boy is sitting on the bench.
③ The girl is standing next to the boy.
④ The dog is sleeping on the tree.

03

다음 대화를 읽고, 물음에 답하세요.

A: ______________________
B: How many?
A: There are ten. Would you like to play soccer tomorrow?
B: That sounds great!

빈칸에 들어갈 말로 가장 알맞은 것을 고르세요.

① There are much balls in the gym.
② There are many balls in the gym.
③ There is many balls in the gym.
④ How many balls are there?

04

다음 그림에 맞게 빈칸에 알맞은 말을 [보기]에서 골라 쓰세요.

[보기] than, more, the, most

A: Look at those shoes! I like those sneakers.
B: I like them, too. But the sneakers are __________ expensive __________ the sandals.

05

다음 그림에 맞도록 빈칸에 들어갈 말을 쓰세요.

A: Look! They're running a race.
B: Wow! Tom is the __________ of them.

06

다음 그림을 보고, 빈칸에 알맞은 단어를 고르세요.

A: Look at the beautiful girl! Do you know her?
B: Yes, I do. She is the __________ beautiful girl in our class.

① than ② most ③ more ④ of

07

다음 그림을 보고, 괄호 안의 단어를 사용하여 비교급 문장이 되도록 알맞은 말을 쓰세요.

Tom is ________ ________ Sam. (tall)

[08~09] 다음 빈칸에 들어갈 알맞은 단어를 쓰세요.

08

A: This steak tastes great.
B: You're right. This is the ________ delicious steak here.

09

A: Look! There is a cat, a lion, and an elephant.
B: Wow! They are different sizes.
A: The elephant is ________ biggest of them.

[10~11] 다음 밑줄 친 부분이 틀린 것을 고르세요.

10

① There are three boys in his room.
② There is some dust in my eyes.
③ Are there apples in the box?
④ Is there a lot of seats in the theater?

11

① Is there a soccer game today?
② There are some money in my pocket.
③ There are many famous buildings.
④ Is there any sugar in the bowl?

[12~14] 우리말 해석과 같은 뜻이 되도록 다음 빈칸에 알맞은 동사를 [보기]에서 골라 쓰세요.

[보기] was, were, are

12
There ________ a snake in the jar yesterday.
(어제 항아리 안에 뱀 한 마리가 있었다.)

13
How many people ________ there in Korea?
(한국에는 얼마나 많은 사람들이 있습니까?)

14
There ________ some flowers in the garden.
(정원에는 약간의 꽃들이 있었다.)

15
다음 중 밑줄 친 부분이 문법에 맞는 문장을 고르세요.

① Are there sugar on the shelf?
② There was a story about the ghost.
③ There were a lot of bread on the table.
④ There is not many people in the park.

[16~18] 다음 문장의 밑줄 친 부분을 바르게 고쳐 문장을 다시 쓰세요.

16
He is the funnyiest in our class.
⇨ ____________________

17
She is beautifuler than you.
⇨ ____________________

18
I am the most fast runner in our class.
⇨ ____________________

[19~20] 우리말 해석과 같도록 괄호 안의 단어를 이용하여 문장을 완성하세요.

19
교실 안에 많은 학생들이 있다.
(many students, in the classroom)
⇨ ____________________

20
벽에 시계가 하나 있다.
(a clock, on the wall)
⇨ ____________________

21

다음 문장을 괄호 안의 문장 종류로 바꾸세요.

Tom was the best student in our class.
(의문문)

⇨ ______________________________

22

밑줄 친 부분을 바르게 고쳐 문장을 다시 쓰세요.

Are there milk in the refrigerator?

⇨ ______________________________

[23~26] 괄호 안의 단어들을 사용하여 우리말 해석과 같도록 비교급 문장을 쓰세요.

23

영어는 한국어보다 어렵다.
(English / difficult / Korean)

⇨ ______________________________

24

서울이 부산보다 크다.
(Seoul / large / Busan)

⇨ ______________________________

25

Tom은 Jack보다 키가 크다. (tall)

⇨ ______________________________

26

영어 시험은 수학 시험보다 쉬웠다.
(exam/ easy)

⇨ ______________________________

[27~30] 괄호 안의 단어들을 사용하여 우리말 해석과 같도록 최상급 문장을 쓰세요.

27

Tom은 가장 똑똑한 학생이다.
(Tom / smart / student)

⇨ ______________________________

28

이 책은 세상에서 가장 비싸다.
(This book / expensive / in the world)

⇨ ______________________________

29

부처는 인도 역사에서 가장 현명한 사람이다.
(Buddha / wise / person / in Indian history)

⇨ ______________________________

30

그는 한국에서 가장 유명한 가수이다.
(famous / singer / in Korea)

⇨ ______________________________

정답 p. 12

Game

아래 그림에 해당하는 단어를 찾아 동그라미 하세요.

R	S	M	B	A	N	A	N	A
W	T	P	Z	L	R	K	X	P
U	B	C	N	Q	U	C	S	P
G	J	H	A	D	M	J	A	L
A	L	E	O	R	A	N	G	E
L	F	E	X	T	R	I	N	Q
D	M	S	W	P	G	O	Z	C
K	I	E	P	O	T	A	T	O

초등영문법3800제 LEVEL 5

워크북

WORKBOOK

1. **단어 쓰기 연습** mp3 음성 파일을 듣고 들려주는 단어를 세 번씩 써 보아요.
2. **Dictation Test** mp3 음성 파일을 듣고 빈칸을 채워 보세요.
3. **단어테스트** 단어 쓰기 연습을 하며 암기한 단어들을 제대로 외웠는지 확인해 보아요.
4. **워크북 정답** Dictation Test와 단어테스트의 정답

초등영문법3800제 MP3 파일 이용 방법

1. 홈페이지에서 다운로드

① 마더텅 홈페이지(www.toptutor.co.kr) 접속 → 상단 메뉴 중 [초등 · 유아]의 [교재 소개] 선택
→ 교재 목록에서 해당 교재명 찾아 선택 → 학습자료의 [mp3] 선택 후 다운로드

② 마더텅 홈페이지(www.toptutor.co.kr) 접속 → 상단 메뉴 중 [초등 · 유아] 의 [교재자료실] 선택
→ 자료실 상단의 [교재를 선택하세요.] 에서 해당 교재명 선택
→ 자료 목록에서 mp3 게시물 선택 후 다운로드

2. 모바일 스트리밍 / 다운로드

① 스마트폰으로 교재 뒷면의 QR코드 스캔 → MP3 스트리밍 or 다운로드

② 주소창에 m.toptutor.co.kr 또는 포털에서 '마더텅' 검색 → [MP3 자료실] 선택
→ 상단 메뉴 중 [초등 · 유아] 선택 → 해당 교재명 찾아 선택 후 MP3 스트리밍 or 다운로드

단어 쓰기 연습 1

초3800_5_w1

들려주는 단어를 잘 듣고, 세 번씩 써 보세요.

MP3 5권 단어 01

01	**fat** ⓗ 뚱뚱한	fat		
02	**sick** ⓗ 아픈	sick		
03	**lovely** ⓗ 사랑스러운	lovely		
04	**liar** ⓜ 거짓말쟁이	liar		
05	**childish** ⓗ 어린애같은	childish		
06	**these** ⓓ 이것들	these		
07	**yummy** ⓗ 맛있는	yummy		
08	**hike** ⓓ 도보여행을 가다	hike		
09	**can** ⓙ ~할 수 있다	can		
10	**should** ⓙ ~해야 한다	should		
11	**will** ⓙ ~할 것이다	will		
12	**from** ⓙ ~로 부터, ~에서	from		
13	**smart** ⓗ 똑똑한	smart		

들려주는 단어를 잘 듣고, 세 번씩 써 보세요.

MP3 5권 단어 01

14 **name** ⓓ ~라고 부르다	name		
15 **fight** ⓓ 싸우다	fight		
16 **each other** ⓓ 서로	each other		
17 **wear** ⓓ 입다	wear		
18 **favorite** ⓗ 가장 좋아하는	favorite		
19 **clothes** ⓜ 옷	clothes		
20 **still** ⓑ 여전히	still		
21 **angry** ⓗ 화난	angry		
22 **concert** ⓜ 콘서트	concert		
23 **academy** ⓜ 학원	academy		
24 **practice** ⓓ 연습하다	practice		
25 **late** ⓗ 늦은	late		
26 **break** ⓓ 부러뜨리다	break		

단어 쓰기 연습 2

초3800_5_w2

들려주는 단어를 잘 듣고, 세 번씩 써 보세요.

MP3 5권 단어 02

27 **leg** 명 다리	leg		
28 **stairs** 명 계단	stairs		
29 **fish** 동 낚시하다	fish		
30 **ski** 동 스키를 타다	ski		
31 **week** 명 주, 일주일	week		
32 **look** 동 ~해 보이다	look		
33 **headache** 명 두통	headache		
34 **boyfriend** 명 남자친구	boyfriend		
35 **boring** 형 지루한	boring		
36 **bake** 동 굽다	bake		
37 **violin** 명 바이올린	violin		
38 **chicken** 명 닭, 치킨	chicken		
39 **salad** 명 샐러드	salad		

들려주는 단어를 잘 듣고, 세 번씩 써 보세요.

MP3 5권 단어 02

40 **cook** ㊎ 요리사	cook		
41 **swim** ㊍ 수영하다	swim		
42 **early** ㊌ 일찍	early		
43 **baseball** ㊎ 야구	baseball		
44 **park** ㊎ 공원	park		
45 **Chinese** ㊎ 중국어	Chinese		
46 **close** ㊍ 닫다	close		
47 **disappointed** ㊏ 실망한	disappointed		
48 **perfect** ㊏ 완벽한	perfect		
49 **fear** ㊍ 두려워하다	fear		
50 **change** ㊎ 변화	change		
51 **alone** ㊏ 혼자인	alone		
52 **clean** ㊏ 깨끗한	clean		

단어 쓰기 연습 3

초3800_5_w3

들려주는 단어를 잘 듣고, 세 번씩 써 보세요.

MP3 5권 단어 03

01 **shoe** 명 신발	shoe		
02 **butter** 명 버터	butter		
03 **cheese** 명 치즈	cheese		
04 **potato** 명 감자	potato		
05 **horse** 명 말	horse		
06 **carrot** 명 당근	carrot		
07 **sand** 명 모래	sand		
08 **tomato** 명 토마토	tomato		
09 **instant** 형 인스턴트의, 즉석의	instant		
10 **noodle** 명 면	noodle		
11 **salt** 명 소금	salt		
12 **lots of** 형 많은	lots of		
13 **mistake** 명 실수	mistake		

들려주는 단어를 잘 듣고, 세 번씩 써 보세요.

MP3 5권 단어 03

14 **banana** ⓜ 바나나	banana		
15 **trash** ⓜ 쓰레기	trash		
16 **sunlight** ⓜ 햇살	sunlight		
17 **pillow** ⓜ 베개	pillow		
18 **spend** ⓢ (시간을) 쓰다	spend		
19 **need** ⓢ 필요하다	need		
20 **supermarket** ⓜ 슈퍼마켓	supermarket		
21 **flour** ⓜ 밀가루	flour		
22 **semester** ⓜ 학기	semester		
23 **begin** ⓢ 시작하다	begin		
24 **bloom** ⓢ 피다	bloom		
25 **grow** ⓢ 키우다	grow		
26 **plant** ⓜ 식물	plant		

단어 쓰기 연습 4

초3800_5_w4

들려주는 단어를 잘 듣고, 세 번씩 써 보세요. MP3 5권 단어 04

27 **yellow** 형 노란 — yellow
28 **dust** 명 먼지 — dust
29 **spring** 명 봄 — spring
30 **beer** 명 맥주 — beer
31 **save** 동 모으다 — save
32 **apple** 명 사과 — apple
33 **find** 동 찾다 — find
34 **ant** 명 개미 — ant
35 **hole** 명 구멍 — hole
36 **pencil** 명 연필 — pencil
37 **uncle** 명 삼촌 — uncle
38 **meat** 명 고기 — meat
39 **pepper** 명 후추 — pepper

들려주는 단어를 잘 듣고, 세 번씩 써 보세요.

MP3 5권 단어 04

40	**balloon** 명 풍선	balloon		
41	**stadium** 명 경기장	stadium		
42	**subject** 명 과목	subject		
43	**stress** 명 스트레스	stress		
44	**worry** 동 걱정하다	worry		
45	**health** 명 건강	health		
46	**bowl** 명 그릇	bowl		
47	**coffee** 명 커피	coffee		
48	**language** 명 언어	language		
49	**question** 명 질문	question		
50	**American** 형 미국의	American		
51	**Coke** 명 콜라	Coke		
52	**light** 형 가벼운	light		

단어 쓰기 연습 5

초3800_5_w5

들려주는 단어를 잘 듣고, 세 번씩 써 보세요.

MP3 5권 단어 **05**

01 **doughnut** 명 도넛	doughnut		
02 **work** 명 일	work		
03 **a few** 형 몇 개의	a few		
04 **cup** 명 컵	cup		
05 **advice** 명 조언	advice		
06 **mushroom** 명 버섯	mushroom		
07 **spark** 명 불꽃	spark		
08 **put** 동 넣다	put		
09 **soup** 명 수프	soup		
10 **order** 동 주문하다	order		
11 **dish** 명 요리	dish		
12 **just** 부 단지	just		
13 **coin** 명 동전	coin		

들려주는 단어를 잘 듣고, 세 번씩 써 보세요.

MP3 5권 단어 05

14 **live** ⓓ 살다	live		
15 **refrigerator** ⓜ 냉장고	refrigerator		
16 **rice** ⓜ 쌀	rice		
17 **cloud** ⓜ 구름	cloud		
18 **milk** ⓜ 우유	milk		
19 **juice** ⓜ 주스	juice		
20 **oil** ⓜ 기름	oil		
21 **desk** ⓜ 책상	desk		
22 **flower** ⓜ 꽃	flower		
23 **leaf** ⓜ 잎	leaf		
24 **a little** ⓗ 약간의	a little		
25 **cut** ⓓ 자르다, 썰다	cut		
26 **cake** ⓜ 케이크	cake		

단어 쓰기 연습 6

초3800_5_w6

들려주는 단어를 잘 듣고, 세 번씩 써 보세요. MP3 5권 단어 06

27 **finish** ⓢ 끝내다	finish		
28 **here** ⓟ 여기에	here		
29 **hour** ⓝ 시간	hour		
30 **onion** ⓝ 양파	onion		
31 **candy** ⓝ 사탕	candy		
32 **use** ⓢ 사용하다	use		
33 **sugar** ⓝ 설탕	sugar		
34 **drink** ⓢ 마시다	drink		
35 **fry** ⓢ 튀기다, 볶다	fry		
36 **classroom** ⓝ 교실	classroom		
37 **sell** ⓢ 팔다	sell		
38 **clothes** ⓝ 옷	clothes		
39 **together** ⓟ 함께	together		

들려주는 단어를 잘 듣고, 세 번씩 써 보세요.

MP3 5권 단어 06

40 **let** ⓢ ~하게 하다	let		
41 **Spanish** ⓜ 스페인어	Spanish		
42 **trouble** ⓜ 문제	trouble		
43 **cousin** ⓜ 사촌	cousin		
44 **exercise** ⓜ 운동	exercise		
45 **winter** ⓜ 겨울	winter		
46 **lose** ⓢ (살이) 빠지다	lose		
47 **night** ⓜ 밤	night		
48 **vegetable** ⓜ 채소	vegetable		
49 **hobby** ⓜ 취미	hobby		
50 **orange** ⓜ 오렌지	orange		
51 **chocolate** ⓜ 초콜릿	chocolate		
52 **harmful** ⓗ 해로운	harmful		

단어 쓰기 연습 7

초3800_5_w7

들려주는 단어를 잘 듣고, 세 번씩 써 보세요.

MP3 5권 단어 07

01 **child** ⓜ 아이	child		
02 **learn** ⓢ 배우다	learn		
03 **stand** ⓢ 서다	stand		
04 **passenger** ⓜ 승객	passenger		
05 **help** ⓜ 도움	help		
06 **think** ⓢ 생각하다	think		
07 **student** ⓜ 학생	student		
08 **lose** ⓢ 잃어버리다	lose		
09 **on** ⓙ ~위에	on		
10 **train** ⓜ 기차	train		
11 **walk** ⓢ 걷다	walk		
12 **weed** ⓜ 잡초	weed		
13 **monkey** ⓜ 원숭이	monkey		

들려주는 단어를 잘 듣고, 세 번씩 써 보세요.

MP3 5권 단어 07

14 **empty** 형 빈	empty		
15 **yummy** 형 맛있는	yummy		
16 **sweet** 명 단 것	sweet		
17 **cold** 형 차가운	cold		
18 **drink** 명 음료	drink		
19 **raw** 형 익히지 않은, 날 것의	raw		
20 **problem** 명 문제	problem		
21 **healthy** 형 건강한	healthy		
22 **for** 전 ~을 위해	for		
23 **cookie** 명 쿠키	cookie		
24 **paint** 동 그리다	paint		
25 **painting** 명 그림	painting		
26 **beautiful** 형 아름다운	beautiful		

단어 쓰기 연습 8

초3800_5_w8

들려주는 단어를 잘 듣고, 세 번씩 써 보세요. MP3 5권 단어 08

27 **praise** ⓢ 칭찬하다	praise		
28 **picture** ⓜ 그림	picture		
29 **everybody** ⓓ 누구든지, 모두	everybody		
30 **pet** ⓜ 애완동물	pet		
31 **park** ⓜ 공원	park		
32 **arrive** ⓢ 도착하다	arrive		
33 **information** ⓜ 정보	information		
34 **steal** ⓢ 훔치다	steal		
35 **money** ⓜ 돈	money		
36 **should** ⓙ ~해야 한다	should		
37 **solution** ⓜ 해결책	solution		
38 **idea** ⓜ 의견, 생각	idea		
39 **ask** ⓢ 질문하다	ask		

들려주는 단어를 잘 듣고, 세 번씩 써 보세요.

MP3 5권 단어 08

40	**lend** ⓢ 빌려주다	lend		
41	**comic book** ⓜ 만화책	comic book		
42	**storybook** ⓜ 이야기책	storybook		
43	**true** ⓗ 진실의, 진짜의	true		
44	**borrow** ⓢ 빌리다	borrow		
45	**children** ⓜ 아이들	children		
46	**starve** ⓢ 굶다	starve		
47	**daughter** ⓜ 딸	daughter		
48	**silver** ⓗ 은색의	silver		
49	**lining** ⓜ 줄무늬	lining		
50	**heal** ⓢ 치료하다	heal		
51	**wound** ⓜ 상처	wound		
52	**basket** ⓜ 바구니	basket		

초3800_5_w9

단어 쓰기 연습 9

들려주는 단어를 잘 듣고, 세 번씩 써 보세요.

MP3 5권 단어 **09**

01 **air conditioner** ㊔ 에어컨	air conditioner		
02 **sofa** ㊔ 소파	sofa		
03 **honey** ㊔ 꿀	honey		
04 **notebook** ㊔ 공책	notebook		
05 **pencil holder** ㊔ 연필꽂이	pencil holder		
06 **colored pencil** ㊔ 색연필	colored pencil		
07 **clip** ㊔ 집게	clip		
08 **paper clip** ㊔ 종이집게	paper clip		
09 **mushroom** ㊔ 버섯	mushroom		
10 **empty** ㊕ 빈	empty		
11 **fresh** ㊕ 신선한	fresh		
12 **strawberry** ㊔ 딸기	strawberry		
13 **broccoli** ㊔ 브로콜리	broccoli		

들려주는 단어를 잘 듣고, 세 번씩 써 보세요.

MP3 5권 단어 09

14 **full** ⓗ 가득 찬	full		
15 **lots of** ⓗ 많은	lots of		
16 **star** ⓜ 별	star		
17 **desk** ⓜ 책상	desk		
18 **clock** ⓜ 시계	clock		
19 **board** ⓜ 판, 판자	board		
20 **enough** ⓗ 충분한	enough		
21 **fight** ⓜ 싸움	fight		
22 **tiger** ⓜ 호랑이	tiger		
23 **lion** ⓜ 사자	lion		
24 **duck** ⓜ 오리	duck		
25 **rabbit** ⓜ 토끼	rabbit		
26 **dolphin** ⓜ 돌고래	dolphin		

단어 쓰기 연습 10

초3800_5_w10

들려주는 단어를 잘 듣고, 세 번씩 써 보세요.　MP3 5권 단어 **10**

27 **monkey** 명 원숭이	monkey			
28 **bird** 명 새	bird			
29 **giraffe** 명 기린	giraffe			
30 **yard** 명 마당	yard			
31 **window** 명 창문	window			
32 **table** 명 탁자	table			
33 **bottle** 명 병	bottle			
34 **hamster** 명 햄스터	hamster			
35 **children** 명 아이들	children			
36 **around** 전 ~의 주위에	around			
37 **delicious** 형 맛있는	delicious			
38 **playground** 명 놀이터	playground			
39 **classroom** 명 교실	classroom			

들려주는 단어를 잘 듣고, 세 번씩 써 보세요.

MP3 5권 단어 10

40 **living room** ⓜ 거실	living room		
41 **here** ⓑ 여기에	here		
42 **juice** ⓜ 주스	juice		
43 **pencil case** ⓜ 필통	pencil case		
44 **light** ⓜ 빛	light		
45 **end** ⓜ 끝	end		
46 **tunnel** ⓜ 터널	tunnel		
47 **chopstick** ⓜ 젓가락	chopstick		
48 **dragonfly** ⓜ 잠자리	dragonfly		
49 **fall** ⓜ 가을	fall		
50 **winter** ⓜ 겨울	winter		
51 **street** ⓜ 길	street		
52 **nap** ⓜ 낮잠	nap		

단어 쓰기 연습 11

초3800_5_w11

들려주는 단어를 잘 듣고, 세 번씩 써 보세요.

MP3 5권 단어 11

01 **turtle** 명 거북이	turtle		
02 **heavy** 형 무거운	heavy		
03 **cheap** 형 싼	cheap		
04 **busy** 형 바쁜	busy		
05 **cheetah** 명 치타	cheetah		
06 **snail** 명 달팽이	snail		
07 **mouse** 명 쥐	mouse		
08 **quietly** 부 조용히	quietly		
09 **other** 대 다른 사람	other		
10 **warm** 형 따뜻한	warm		
11 **rent** 명 집세, 방세	rent		
12 **soon** 부 빨리	soon		
13 **low** 형 낮은	low		

들려주는 단어를 잘 듣고, 세 번씩 써 보세요.

MP3 5권 단어 11

14 **famous** ⓗ 유명한	famous		
15 **studio** ⓜ 촬영장	studio		
16 **long** ⓑ 오래	long		
17 **quickly** ⓑ 빠르게	quickly		
18 **when** ⓙ ~할 때	when		
19 **interesting** ⓗ 재미있는	interesting		
20 **airplane** ⓜ 비행기	airplane		
21 **noisy** ⓗ 시끄러운	noisy		
22 **taxi** ⓜ 택시	taxi		
23 **expensive** ⓗ 비싼	expensive		
24 **comfortable** ⓗ 편안한	comfortable		
25 **expect** ⓓ 기대하다	expect		
26 **motorcycle** ⓜ 오토바이	motorcycle		

단어 쓰기 연습 12

초3800_5_w12

들려주는 단어를 잘 듣고, 세 번씩 써 보세요.

MP3 5권 단어 12

27 **dangerous** 형 위험한	dangerous		
28 **lemon** 명 레몬	lemon		
29 **sour** 형 신	sour		
30 **orange** 명 오렌지	orange		
31 **important** 형 중요한	important		
32 **friendship** 명 우정	friendship		
33 **brave** 형 용감한	brave		
34 **believe** 동 믿다	believe		
35 **be born** 동 태어나다	be born		
36 **blood** 명 피	blood		
37 **thick** 형 진한	thick		
38 **pen** 명 펜	pen		
39 **mighty** 형 강한	mighty		

들려주는 단어를 잘 듣고, 세 번씩 써 보세요.

MP3 5권 단어 12

40 **sword** 명 칼	sword		
41 **action** 명 행동	action		
42 **word** 명 단어, 말	word		
43 **neighbor** 명 이웃	neighbor		
44 **distant** 형 먼	distant		
45 **notebook** 명 공책	notebook		
46 **navy** 형 남색의	navy		
47 **white** 형 흰색의	white		
48 **pants** 명 바지	pants		
49 **shirt** 명 셔츠	shirt		
50 **adult** 명 어른	adult		
51 **high** 형 높은	high		
52 **mark** 명 점수	mark		

단어 쓰기 연습 13

초3800_5_w13

들려주는 단어를 잘 듣고, 세 번씩 써 보세요.

MP3 5권 단어 13

01	**wide**	(형) 넓은	wide
02	**lucky**	(형) 운이 좋은	lucky
03	**animal**	(명) 동물	animal
04	**class**	(명) 반	class
05	**thin**	(형) 가는	thin
06	**watermelon**	(명) 수박	watermelon
07	**hard**	(형) 어려운	hard
08	**slowly**	(부) 느리게	slowly
09	**difficult**	(형) 어려운	difficult
10	**surprising**	(형) 놀라운	surprising
11	**singer**	(명) 가수	singer
12	**get**	(동) 얻다	get
13	**score**	(명) 점수	score

들려주는 단어를 잘 듣고, 세 번씩 써 보세요.

MP3 5권 단어 13

14 **test** 명 시험	test		
15 **camel** 명 낙타	camel		
16 **pig** 명 돼지	pig		
17 **parrot** 명 앵무새	parrot		
18 **meaningful** 형 의미있는	meaningful		
19 **January** 명 1월	January		
20 **short** 형 짧은	short		
21 **exciting** 형 신나는	exciting		
22 **island** 명 섬	island		
23 **also** 부 ~도, 또한	also		
24 **mountain** 명 산	mountain		
25 **grill** 동 석쇠로 굽다	grill		
26 **black** 형 검은	black		

단어 쓰기 연습 14

초3800_5_w14

들려주는 단어를 잘 듣고, 세 번씩 써 보세요.

MP3 5권 단어 14

27 **pork** ⓜ 돼지고기	pork		
28 **ride** ⓜ 놀이기구	ride		
29 **boring** ⓗ 지루한	boring		
30 **merry-go-round** ⓜ 회전목마	merry-go-round		
31 **special** ⓗ 특별한	special		
32 **popular** ⓗ 인기있는	popular		
33 **kingdom** ⓜ 왕국	kingdom		
34 **vote** ⓜ 표	vote		
35 **diligent** ⓗ 성실한, 부지런한	diligent		
36 **restaurant** ⓜ 레스토랑	restaurant		
37 **city** ⓜ 도시	city		
38 **steak** ⓜ 스테이크	steak		
39 **honesty** ⓜ 정직	honesty		

들려주는 단어를 잘 듣고, 세 번씩 써 보세요.

MP3 5권 단어 14

40 **fearful** ㊌ 무서운	fearful		
41 **subject** ㊐ 과목	subject		
42 **order** ㊍ 주문하다	order		
43 **dish** ㊐ 요리	dish		
44 **step** ㊐ 걸음	step		
45 **potential** ㊐ 가능성	potential		
46 **voice** ㊐ 목소리	voice		
47 **trait** ㊐ 특징	trait		
48 **choice** ㊐ 선택	choice		
49 **world** ㊐ 세상	world		
50 **song** ㊐ 노래	song		
51 **kind** ㊌ 친절한	kind		
52 **noisy** ㊌ 시끄러운	noisy		

초3800_5_d1

Dictation Test 1

MP3 5권 받아쓰기 **01**

Name : **Date :** **Score :** /10

[01~10] 들려주는 문장을 잘 듣고 빈칸에 알맞은 단어를 채워 보세요.

01. Mina is smart, ______ ______?
미나는 똑똑해, 그렇지 않아?

02. He is not fat, ______ ______?
그는 뚱뚱하지 않아, 그렇지?

03. Sihu was late for school, ______ ______?
시후는 학교에 늦었어, 그렇지 않아?

04. Nayeon is still angry, ______ ______?
나연이는 여전히 화가 나있어, 그렇지 않아?

05. This book is boring, ______ ______?
이 책은 지루해, 그렇지 않니?

06. We are not alone, ______ ______?
우리는 혼자가 아니야, 그렇지?

07. Chinese isn't easy, ______ ______?
중국어는 쉽지 않아, 그렇지?

08. He was disappointed, ______ ______?
그는 실망했어, 그렇지 않아?

09. Her mother was a teacher, ______ ______?
그녀의 엄마는 선생님이셨어, 그렇지 않아?

10. They are twins, ______ ______?
그들은 쌍둥이야, 그렇지 않니?

정답 p.230

초3800_5_d2

Dictation Test 2

MP3 5권 받아쓰기 02

Name : Date : Score : /10

[01~10] 들려주는 문장을 잘 듣고 빈칸에 알맞은 단어를 채워 보세요.

01. You won't forget me, __________ __________?
너는 나를 잊지 않을 거야, 그렇지?

02. They fought last night, __________ __________?
그들은 어젯밤에 싸웠어, 그렇지 않아?

03. You don't know the answer, __________ __________?
너는 답을 몰라, 그렇지?

04. You can play the piano, __________ __________?
너는 피아노를 칠 수 있어, 그렇지 않아?

05. You will practice hard, __________ __________?
너는 열심히 연습할 거야, 그렇지 않아?

06. He didn't wake up late, __________ __________?
그는 늦게 일어나지 않았어, 그렇지?

07. She doesn't have a headache, __________ __________?
그녀는 두통이 있지 않잖아, 그렇지?

08. She can play the violin, __________ __________?
그녀는 바이올린을 연주할 수 있어, 그렇지 않아?

09. They will go fishing, __________ __________?
그들은 낚시하러 갈 거야, 그렇지 않니?

10. Clara can't swim well, __________ __________?
Clara는 수영을 잘 하지 못해, 그렇지?

정답 p.230

초3800_5_d3

Dictation Test 3

MP3 5권 받아쓰기 03

Name : Date : Score : /10

[01~10] 들려주는 문장을 잘 듣고 빈칸에 알맞은 단어를 채워 보세요.

01. We have ________________ dishes.
우리는 많은 그릇들을 갖고 있어.

02. His mom bought ________________ pillows.
그의 엄마는 많은 베개들을 샀어.

03. I don't need ________________ butter.
나는 많은 버터가 필요하지 않아.

04. I used too ________________ flour.
나는 너무 많은 밀가루를 썼어.

05. ________________ flowers began to bloom.
많은 꽃들이 피기 시작했어.

06. He eats too ________________ pepper.
그는 너무 많은 후추를 먹어.

07. I didn't take ________________ rest.
나는 많은 휴식을 취하지 못했어.

08. She learns ________________ languages.
그녀는 많은 언어들을 배워.

09. ________________ drops make a shower.
많은 빗방울들이 모여 소나기를 만든다. (티끌모아 태산이다.)

10. We don't have ________________ time.
우리는 시간이 많지 않아.

정답 p.230

초3800_5_d4

Dictation Test 4

MP3 5권 받아쓰기 04

Name : Date : Score : /10

[01~10] 들려주는 문장을 잘 듣고 빈칸에 알맞은 단어를 채워 보세요.

01. They drank ________________ beer yesterday.
그들은 어제 많은 맥주를 마셨어.

02. Ice cream has ________________ sugar.
아이스크림에는 많은 설탕이 들어있어.

03. She heard ________________ good news.
그녀는 많은 좋은 소식들을 들었어.

04. We took ________________ photos.
우리는 많은 사진들을 찍었어.

05. I have ________________ stress.
나 스트레스 많이 받아.

06. I could see ________________ people at the stadium.
나는 경기장에서 많은 사람들을 볼 수 있었어.

07. Did you spend ________________ time with her?
너는 그녀와 많은 시간을 함께 보냈니?

08. He drinks ________________ Coke.
그는 많은 콜라를 마셔.

09. Mother Teresa helped ________________ people.
테레사 수녀는 많은 사람들을 도왔어.

10. She has ________________ pencils.
그녀는 많은 연필들을 갖고 있어.

정답 p.230

초3800_5_d5

Dictation Test 5

MP3 5권 받아쓰기 05

Name : Date : Score : /10

[01~10] 들려주는 문장을 잘 듣고 빈칸에 알맞은 단어를 채워 보세요.

01. I need ________________ onions.
나는 양파 몇 개가 필요해.

02. Sihu drinks ________________ milk.
시후는 약간의 우유를 마셔.

03. I used ________________ eggs.
나는 계란 몇 개를 사용했어.

04. I cut ________________ vegetables.
나는 야채 몇 개를 썰었어.

05. I fried ________________ meat.
나는 조금의 고기를 볶았어.

06. I finished ________________ homework.
나는 숙제 몇 개를 끝냈어.

07. She has ________________ money.
그녀는 약간의 돈이 있어.

08. I have ________________ troubles.
나는 문제가 조금 있어요.

09. We need ________________ salt.
우리는 조금의 소금이 필요해.

10. I have ________________ hobbies.
나는 취미가 몇 개 있어.

정답 p.230

소3800_5_d6

Dictation Test 6

MP3 5권 받아쓰기 06

Name : Date : Score : /10

[01~10] 들려주는 문장을 잘 듣고 빈칸에 알맞은 단어를 채워 보세요.

01. He drinks ________________ water.
그는 물을 거의 마시지 않아.

02. We eat ________________ candies.
우리는 사탕을 거의 먹지 않아.

03. There was ________________ rice.
밥이 거의 없었어.

04. They had ________________ time.
그들은 시간이 거의 없었어.

05. My dad eats ________________ meat.
나의 아빠는 고기를 거의 드시지 않아.

06. They read ________________ books.
그들은 책을 거의 읽지 않았어.

07. I eat ________________ vegetables.
나는 야채를 거의 먹지 않아.

08. We spent ________________ time together.
우리는 함께 보낸 시간이 거의 없었어요.

09. I have ________________ clothes.
나는 옷이 거의 없어요.

10. I have ________________ homework now.
나는 이제 숙제가 거의 없어.

정답 p.230

초3800_5_d7

Dictation Test 7

MP3 5권 받아쓰기 07

Name : Date : Score : /10

[01~10] 들려주는 문장을 잘 듣고 빈칸에 알맞은 단어를 채워 보세요.

01. I don't want ________________ sweets.
나는 단 것들을 조금도 원하지 않아.

02. Can I drink ________________ milk?
내가 우유를 좀 먹어도 될까?

03. Do you have ________________ pets?
너 애완동물 키워?

04. Can I borrow ________________ rice?
제가 쌀을 좀 빌릴 수 있을까요?

05. Is there ________________ problem?
무슨 문제 있니?

06. I read ________________ webtoons.
나는 웹툰 몇 개를 읽었어.

07. Can I have ________________ Coke?
저 콜라 좀 먹어도 돼요?

08. Do you have ________________ questions?
질문들이 좀 있나요?

09. We should find ________________ solutions.
우리는 해결책을 좀 찾아야 해.

10. I don't have ________________ storybooks.
나는 이야기책이 하나도 없어.

정답 p.230

Dictation Test 8

초3800_5_d8

MP3 5권 받아쓰기 08

Name : Date : Score : /10

[01~10] 들려주는 문장을 잘 듣고 빈칸에 알맞은 단어를 채워 보세요.

01. I paint ________________ Saturday.
나는 매주 토요일마다 그림을 그려.

02. ________________ my paintings are beautiful.
나의 모든 그림들은 아름다워.

03. ________________ my dreams will come true.
내 모든 꿈들이 이루어질 거야.

04. ________________ student passed the exam.
모든 학생들이 시험을 통과했어.

05. ________________ cloud has a silver lining.
모든 구름은 은빛 테두리(구름 뒤 햇살)가 있다. (어려운 상황에도 희망은 있다.)

06. Time heals ________________ wounds.
시간은 모든 상처를 치유한다. (시간이 약이다.)

07. ________________ child needs friends.
모든 아이들은 친구들이 필요해.

08. No way! ________________ vegetables taste bad!
그럴 리가! 모든 채소들은 맛없어!

09. I read two books ________________ week.
나는 매주 두 권의 책을 읽어.

10. ________________ mother loves her daughter.
모든 엄마들은 그녀의 딸을 사랑해.

정답 p.230

초3800_5_d9

Dictation Test 9

MP3 5권 받아쓰기 **09**

Name : Date : Score : /10

[01~10] 들려주는 문장을 잘 듣고 빈칸에 알맞은 단어를 채워 보세요.

01. ________ ________ one big lion.
한 마리의 큰 사자가 있어.

02. ________ ________ many ducks in the pond.
연못에 많은 오리들이 있어.

03. ________ ________ a bird in the tree.
나무에는 새 한 마리가 있어.

04. ________ ________ two children.
두 명의 어린이들이 있어.

05. ________ ________ three dogs in the yard.
마당에는 세 마리의 개가 있어.

06. ________ ________ juice in the bottle.
병에는 주스가 있어.

07. ________ ________ a cat on the street.
길 위에 고양이 한 마리가 있어.

08. ________ ________ a piece of cake.
케이크 한 조각이 있어.

09. ________ ________ many dragonflies in the fall.
가을에는 많은 잠자리들이 있어.

10. ________ ________ many friends around you.
네 주위에는 많은 친구들이 있어.

정답 **p.230**

초3800_5_d10

Dictation Test 10

MP3 5권 받아쓰기 10

Name : Date : Score : /10

[01~10] 들려주는 문장을 잘 듣고 빈칸에 알맞은 단어를 채워 보세요.

01. ____________ ____________ a lot of rabbits?
많은 토끼들이 있니?

02. ____________ ____________ a tree here now.
지금은 여기에 나무 한 그루가 없어.

03. ____________ ____________ much milk in the bottle?
병에 우유가 많니?

04. ____________ ____________ not a child in the playground.
놀이터에는 아이가 없었어.

05. ____________ ____________ many dogs in the park?
공원에 개들이 많이 있어?

06. ____________ ____________ no wind yesterday.
어제 바람 한 점 없었어.

07. ____________ ____________ any chopsticks?
젓가락 있니?

08. ____________ ____________ a subway station near your house?
당신의 집 근처에 지하철역이 있나요?

09. ____________ ____________ not a student here.
이곳에는 학생이 없어.

10. ____________ ____________ dogs in your home?
너희 집에 개들이 있니?

정답 p.230

초3800_5_d11

Dictation Test 11

MP3 5권 받아쓰기 **11**

Name : Date : Score : /10

[01~10] 들려주는 문장을 잘 듣고 빈칸에 알맞은 단어를 채워 보세요.

01. Seoul is ______________ than Busan.
서울은 부산보다 추워.

02. Boni is ______________ than Hani.
보니는 하니보다 키가 커.

03. The turtle is ______________ than the rabbit.
그 거북이는 그 토끼보다 나이가 많아.

04. A rabbit runs ______________ than a turtle.
토끼는 거북이보다 빨리 달려.

05. A turtle lives ______________ than a rabbit.
거북이는 토끼보다 오래 살아.

06. The baby is ______________ than his brother.
그 아기는 그의 형보다 더 작아.

07. Blood is ______________ than water.
피는 물보다 진하다.

08. Is she ______________ than me?
그녀가 나보다 예뻐?

09. Fruits are ______________ than vegetables.
과일은 채소보다 더 달아.

10. A watermelon is ______________ than a melon.
수박은 메론보다 더 무거워.

정답 p.230

초3800_5_d12

Dictation Test 12

MP3 5권 받아쓰기 12

Name : Date : Score : /10

[01~10] 들려주는 문장을 잘 듣고 빈칸에 알맞은 단어를 채워 보세요.

01. I think Busan is ________ ________ than Seoul.
나는 부산이 서울보다 더 아름답다고 생각해.

02. I like movies ________ than books.
나는 책보다 영화가 더 좋아.

03. A movie is ________ ________ than a book.
영화는 책보다 흥미로워.

04. Hani is ________ ________ than Boni.
하니는 보니보다 유명해.

05. Children learn English ________ ________ than adults.
아이들은 어른들보다 영어를 더 빨리 배워.

06. Two heads are ________ than one.
하나보다는 둘이 더 낫다. (백지장도 맞들면 낫다.)

07. I am ________ this year than last year.
나는 작년보다 올해 더 뚱뚱하다.

08. I am ________ ________ than yesterday.
나는 어제보다 더 피곤해.

09. A motorcycle is ________ ________ than a car.
오토바이가 자동차보다 더 위험해.

10. Math is ________ ________ than English.
수학은 영어보다 더 어려워.

정답 p.230

초3800_5_d13

Dictation Test 13

MP3 5권 받아쓰기 13

Name : Date : Score : /10

[01~10] 들려주는 문장을 잘 듣고 빈칸에 알맞은 단어를 채워 보세요.

01. This is the ________________ lion.
이건 가장 빠른 사자야.

02. The giraffe is the ________________ animal.
기린은 가장 키가 큰 동물이야.

03. We have the ________________ parrot.
우리는 가장 똑똑한 앵무새를 갖고 있어.

04. Is it the ________________ roller coaster in Korea?
이게 한국에서 가장 긴 롤러코스터야?

05. He is the ________________ boy on my team.
그는 우리 팀에서 가장 친절한 남자아이야.

06. My little brother is the ________________ in the world!
내 남동생은 세상에서 제일 귀여워!

07. I will be the ________________ sister of all.
나는 가장 멋진 누나가 될 거야.

08. It was the ________________ moment in my life.
그건 내 인생에서 가장 행복한 순간이었어.

09. My grandfather is the ________________ in my family.
나의 할아버지는 우리 가족 중에서 제일 나이가 많으셔.

10. The first step is always the ________________.
첫 걸음은 항상 가장 어렵다.

정답 p.230

초3800_5_d14

Dictation Test 14

MP3 5권 받아쓰기 14

Name : Date : Score : /10

[01~10] 들려주는 문장을 잘 듣고 빈칸에 알맞은 단어를 채워 보세요.

01. That is the ______________ camel.
저건 가장 큰 낙타야.

02. I saw the ______________ pig.
나는 가장 뚱뚱한 돼지를 봤어.

03. Jeju Island is the ______________ ______________ island in Korea.
제주도는 한국에서 가장 아름다운 섬이야.

04. It is the ______________ ______________ ride.
그건 가장 인기 있는 놀이기구야.

05. English is the ______________ ______________ subject!
영어는 가장 어려운 과목이야!

06. That man is the ______________ ______________ actor on stage.
저 남자는 무대에서 가장 잘생긴 배우야.

07. This is the ______________ movie!
이건 최악의 영화야!

08. This is the ______________ ______________ play!
이건 가장 재밌는 연극이야!

09. You got the ______________ votes.
너는 가장 많은 표를 받았어.

10. This computer is the ______________ in the store.
이 컴퓨터는 가게 안에서 가장 좋아.

정답 p.230

단어테스트 1

다음 한글 뜻을 보고 영어 표현을 적으세요. Name : Date : Score : /26

번호	답	뜻	번호	답	뜻
01		형 뚱뚱한	14		동 ~라고 부르다
02		형 아픈	15		동 싸우다
03		형 사랑스러운	16		대 서로
04		명 거짓말쟁이	17		동 입다
05		형 어린애같은	18		형 가장 좋아하는
06		대 이것들	19		명 옷
07		형 맛있는	20		부 여전히
08		동 도보여행을 가다	21		형 화난
09		조 ~할 수 있다	22		명 콘서트
10		조 ~해야 한다	23		명 학원
11		조 ~할 것이다	24		동 연습하다
12		전 ~로 부터, ~에서	25		형 늦은
13		형 똑똑한	26		동 부러뜨리다

정답 p.230

단어테스트 2

다음 한글 뜻을 보고 영어 표현을 적으세요. Name : Date : Score : /26

01		명 다리	14		명 요리사
02		명 계단	15		동 수영하다
03		동 낚시하다	16		부 일찍
04		동 스키를 타다	17		명 야구
05		명 주, 일주일	18		명 공원
06		동 ~해 보이다	19		명 중국어
07		명 두통	20		동 닫다
08		명 남자친구	21		형 실망한
09		형 지루한	22		형 완벽한
10		동 굽다	23		동 두려워하다
11		명 바이올린	24		명 변화
12		명 닭, 치킨	25		형 혼자인
13		명 샐러드	26		형 깨끗한

정답 p.230

단어테스트 3

다음 한글 뜻을 보고 영어 표현을 적으세요. Name : Date : Score : /26

01		명 신발	14		명 바나나
02		명 버터	15		명 쓰레기
03		명 치즈	16		명 햇살
04		명 감자	17		명 베개
05		명 말	18		동 (시간을) 쓰다
06		명 당근	19		동 필요하다
07		명 모래	20		명 슈퍼마켓
08		명 토마토	21		명 밀가루
09		형 인스턴트의, 즉석의	22		명 학기
10		명 면	23		동 시작하다
11		명 소금	24		동 피다
12		형 많은	25		동 키우다
13		명 실수	26		명 식물

정답 p.230

단어테스트 4

다음 한글 뜻을 보고 영어 표현을 적으세요. Name : Date : Score : /26

01		형 노란	14		명 풍선
02		명 먼지	15		명 경기장
03		명 봄	16		명 과목
04		명 맥주	17		명 스트레스
05		동 모으다	18		동 걱정하다
06		명 사과	19		명 건강
07		동 찾다	20		명 그릇
08		명 개미	21		명 커피
09		명 구멍	22		명 언어
10		명 연필	23		명 질문
11		명 삼촌	24		형 미국의
12		명 고기	25		명 콜라
13		명 후추	26		형 가벼운

정답 p.230

단어테스트

단어테스트 5

다음 한글 뜻을 보고 영어 표현을 적으세요. Name : Date : Score : /26

01	⑲ 도넛	14	⑤ 살다
02	⑲ 일	15	⑲ 냉장고
03	⑱ 몇 개의	16	⑲ 쌀
04	⑲ 컵	17	⑲ 구름
05	⑲ 조언	18	⑲ 우유
06	⑲ 버섯	19	⑲ 주스
07	⑲ 불꽃	20	⑲ 기름
08	⑤ 넣다	21	⑲ 책상
09	⑲ 수프	22	⑲ 꽃
10	⑤ 주문하다	23	⑲ 잎
11	⑲ 요리	24	⑱ 약간의
12	⑮ 단지	25	⑤ 자르다, 썰다
13	⑲ 동전	26	⑲ 케이크

정답 p.231

단어테스트 6

다음 한글 뜻을 보고 영어 표현을 적으세요. Name : Date : Score : /26

01		동 끝내다	14		동 ~하게 하다
02		부 여기에	15		명 스페인어
03		명 시간	16		명 문제
04		명 양파	17		명 사촌
05		명 사탕	18		명 운동
06		동 사용하다	19		명 겨울
07		명 설탕	20		동 (살이) 빠지다
08		동 마시다	21		명 밤
09		동 튀기다, 볶다	22		명 채소
10		명 교실	23		명 취미
11		동 팔다	24		명 오렌지
12		명 옷	25		명 초콜릿
13		부 함께	26		형 해로운

정답 p.231

단어테스트 7

다음 한글 뜻을 보고 영어 표현을 적으세요. Name : Date : Score : /26

01		명 아이	14		형 빈
02		동 배우다	15		형 맛있는
03		동 서다	16		명 단 것
04		명 승객	17		형 차가운
05		명 도움	18		명 음료
06		동 생각하다	19		형 익히지 않은, 날 것의
07		명 학생	20		명 문제
08		동 잃어버리다	21		형 건강한
09		전 ~위에	22		전 ~을 위해
10		명 기차	23		명 쿠키
11		동 걷다	24		동 그리다
12		명 잡초	25		명 그림
13		명 원숭이	26		형 아름다운

정답 p.231

단어테스트 8

다음 한글 뜻을 보고 영어 표현을 적으세요. Name : Date : Score : /26

01			동 칭찬하다
02			명 그림
03			대 누구든지, 모두
04			명 애완동물
05			명 공원
06			동 도착하다
07			명 정보
08			동 훔치다
09			명 돈
10			조 ~해야 한다
11			명 해결책
12			명 의견, 생각
13			동 질문하다
14			동 빌려주다
15			명 만화책
16			명 이야기책
17			형 진실의, 진짜의
18			동 빌리다
19			명 아이들
20			동 굶다
21			명 딸
22			형 은색의
23			명 줄무늬
24			동 치료하다
25			명 상처
26			명 바구니

정답 p.231

단어테스트 9

다음 한글 뜻을 보고 영어 표현을 적으세요. Name : Date : Score : /26

01		명 에어컨	14		형 가득 찬
02		명 소파	15		형 많은
03		명 꿀	16		명 별
04		명 공책	17		명 책상
05		명 연필꽂이	18		명 시계
06		명 색연필	19		명 판, 판자
07		명 집게	20		형 충분한
08		명 종이집게	21		명 싸움
09		명 버섯	22		명 호랑이
10		형 빈	23		명 사자
11		형 신선한	24		명 오리
12		명 딸기	25		명 토끼
13		명 브로콜리	26		명 돌고래

정답 p.231

단어테스트 10

다음 한글 뜻을 보고 영어 표현을 적으세요. Name : Date : Score : /26

01		명 원숭이	14		명 거실
02		명 새	15		부 여기에
03		명 기린	16		명 주스
04		명 마당	17		명 필통
05		명 창문	18		명 빗
06		명 탁자	19		명 끝
07		명 병	20		명 터널
08		명 햄스터	21		명 젓가락
09		명 아이들	22		명 잠자리
10		전 ~의 주위에	23		명 가을
11		형 맛있는	24		명 겨울
12		명 놀이터	25		명 길
13		명 교실	26		명 낮잠

정답 p.231

단어테스트 11

다음 한글 뜻을 보고 영어 표현을 적으세요. Name : Date : Score : /26

01		명 거북이	
02		형 무거운	
03		형 싼	
04		형 바쁜	
05		명 치타	
06		명 달팽이	
07		명 쥐	
08		부 조용히	
09		대 다른 사람	
10		형 따뜻한	
11		명 집세, 방세	
12		부 빨리	
13		형 낮은	
14		형 유명한	
15		명 촬영장	
16		부 오래	
17		부 빠르게	
18		접 ~할 때	
19		형 재미있는	
20		명 비행기	
21		형 시끄러운	
22		명 택시	
23		형 비싼	
24		형 편안한	
25		동 기대하다	
26		명 오토바이	

정답 p.231

단어테스트 12

다음 한글 뜻을 보고 영어 표현을 적으세요. Name : Date : Score : /26

번호	답	뜻	번호	답	뜻
01		형 위험한	14		명 칼
02		명 레몬	15		명 행동
03		형 신	16		명 단어, 말
04		명 오렌지	17		명 이웃
05		형 중요한	18		형 먼
06		명 우정	19		명 공책
07		형 용감한	20		형 남색의
08		동 믿다	21		형 흰색의
09		동 태어나다	22		명 바지
10		명 피	23		명 셔츠
11		형 진한	24		명 어른
12		명 펜	25		형 높은
13		형 강한	26		명 점수

정답 p.231

단어테스트 13

다음 한글 뜻을 보고 영어 표현을 적으세요. Name : Date : Score : /26

01		형 넓은	14		명 시험
02		형 운이 좋은	15		명 낙타
03		명 동물	16		명 돼지
04		명 반	17		명 앵무새
05		형 가는	18		형 의미있는
06		명 수박	19		명 1월
07		형 어려운	20		형 짧은
08		부 느리게	21		형 신나는
09		형 어려운	22		명 섬
10		형 놀라운	23		부 ~도, 또한
11		명 가수	24		명 산
12		동 얻다	25		동 석쇠로 굽다
13		명 점수	26		형 검은

정답 p.231

단어테스트 14

다음 한글 뜻을 보고 영어 표현을 적으세요. Name : Date : Score : /26

01		명 돼지고기	14		형 무서운
02		명 놀이기구	15		명 과목
03		형 지루한	16		동 주문하다
04		명 회전목마	17		명 요리
05		형 특별한	18		명 걸음
06		형 인기있는	19		명 가능성
07		명 왕국	20		명 목소리
08		명 표	21		명 특징
09		형 성실한, 부지런한	22		명 선택
10		명 레스토랑	23		명 세상
11		명 도시	24		명 노래
12		명 스테이크	25		형 친절한
13		명 정직	26		형 시끄러운

정답 p.231

워크북 정답

Dictation Test 1

01. isn't, she
02. is, he
03. wasn't, he
04. isn't, she
05. isn't, it
06. are, we
07. is, it
08. wasn't, he
09. wasn't, she
10. aren't, they

Dictation Test 2

01. will, you
02. didn't, they
03. do, you
04. can't, you
05. won't, you
06. did, he
07. does, she
08. can't, she
09. won't, they
10. can, she

Dictation Test 3

01. many
02. many
03. much
04. much
05. Many
06. much
07. much
08. many
09. Many
10. much

Dictation Test 4

01. a lot of
02. lots of
03. a lot of
04. a lot of
05. a lot of
06. lots of
07. a lot of
08. lots of
09. a lot of
10. a lot of

Dictation Test 5

01. a few
02. a little
03. a few
04. a few
05. a little
06. a little
07. a little
08. a few
09. a little
10. a few

Dictation Test 6

01. little
02. few
03. little
04. little
05. little
06. few
07. few
08. little
09. few
10. little

Dictation Test 7

01. any
02. some
03. any
04. some
05. any
06. some
07. some
08. any
09. some
10. any

Dictation Test 8

01. every
02. All
03. All
04. Every
05. Every
06. all
07. Every
08. All
09. every
10. Every

Dictation Test 9

01. There, is
02. There, are
03. There, is
04. There, are
05. There, are
06. There, is
07. There, is
08. There, is
09. There, are
10. There, are

Dictation Test 10

01. Are, there
02. There, isn't
03. Is, there
04. There, was
05. Are, there
06. There, was
07. Are, there
08. Is, there
09. There, is
10. Are, there

Dictation Test 11

01. colder
02. taller
03. older
04. faster
05. longer
06. smaller
07. thicker
08. prettier
09. sweeter
10. heavier

Dictation Test 12

01. more, beautiful
02. better
03. more, interesting
04. more, famous
05. more, quickly
06. better
07. fatter
08. more, tired
09. more, dangerous
10. more, difficult

Dictation Test 13

01. fastest
02. tallest
03. smartest
04. longest
05. kindest
06. cutest
07. nicest
08. happiest
09. oldest
10. hardest

Dictation Test 14

01. biggest
02. fattest
03. most, beautiful
04. most, popular
05. most, difficult
06. most, handsome
07. worst
08. most, interesting
09. most
10. best

단어테스트 1

01. fat
02. sick
03. lovely
04. liar
05. childish
06. these
07. yummy
08. hike
09. can
10. should
11. will
12. from
13. smart
14. name
15. fight
16. each other
17. wear
18. favorite
19. clothes
20. still
21. angry
22. concert
23. academy
24. practice
25. late
26. break

단어테스트 2

01. leg
02. stairs
03. fish
04. ski
05. week
06. look
07. headache
08. boyfriend
09. boring
10. bake
11. violin
12. chicken
13. salad
14. cook
15. swim
16. early
17. baseball
18. park
19. Chinese
20. close
21. disappointed
22. perfect
23. fear
24. change
25. alone
26. clean

단어테스트 3

01. shoe
02. butter
03. cheese
04. potato
05. horse
06. carrot
07. sand
08. tomato
09. instant
10. noodle
11. salt
12. lots of
13. mistake
14. banana
15. trash
16. sunlight
17. pillow
18. spend
19. need
20. supermarket
21. flour
22. semester
23. begin
24. bloom
25. grow
26. plant

단어테스트 4

01. yellow
02. dust
03. spring
04. beer
05. save
06. apple
07. find

08. ant
09. hole
10. pencil
11. uncle
12. meat
13. pepper
14. balloon
15. stadium
16. subject
17. stress
18. worry
19. health
20. bowl
21. coffee
22. language
23. question
24. American
25. Coke
26. light

단어테스트 5

01. doughnut
02. work
03. a few
04. cup
05. advice
06. mushroom
07. spark
08. put
09. soup
10. order
11. dish
12. just
13. coin
14. live
15. refrigerator
16. rice
17. cloud
18. milk
19. juice
20. oil
21. desk
22. flower
23. leaf
24. a little
25. cut
26. cake

단어테스트 6

01. finish
02. here
03. hour
04. onion
05. candy
06. use
07. sugar

08. drink
09. fry
10. classroom
11. sell
12. clothes
13. together
14. let
15. Spanish
16. trouble
17. cousin
18. exercise
19. winter
20. lose
21. night
22. vegetable
23. hobby
24. orange
25. chocolate
26. harmful

단어테스트 7

01. child
02. learn
03. stand
04. passenger
05. help
06. think
07. student
08. lose
09. on
10. train
11. walk
12. weed
13. monkey
14. empty
15. yummy
16. sweet
17. cold
18. drink
19. raw
20. problem
21. healthy
22. for
23. cookie
24. paint
25. painting
26. beautiful

단어테스트 8

01. praise
02. picture
03. everybody
04. pet
05. park
06. arrive
07. information

08. steal
09. money
10. should
11. solution
12. idea
13. ask
14. lend
15. comic book
16. storybook
17. true
18. borrow
19. children
20. starve
21. daughter
22. silver
23. lining
24. heal
25. wound
26. basket

단어테스트 9

01. air conditioner
02. sofa
03. honey
04. notebook
05. pencil holder
06. colored pencil
07. clip
08. paper clip
09. mushroom
10. empty
11. fresh
12. strawberry
13. broccoli
14. full
15. lots of
16. star
17. desk
18. clock
19. board
20. enough
21. fight
22. tiger
23. lion
24. duck
25. rabbit
26. dolphin

단어테스트 10

01. monkey
02. bird
03. giraffe
04. yard
05. window
06. table
07. bottle

08. hamster
09. children
10. around
11. delicious
12. playground
13. classroom
14. living room
15. here
16. juice
17. pencil case
18. light
19. end
20. tunnel
21. chopstick
22. drangonfly
23. fall
24. winter
25. street
26. nap

단어테스트 11

01. turtle
02. heavy
03. cheap
04. busy
05. cheetah
06. snail
07. mouse
08. quietly
09. other
10. warm
11. rent
12. soon
13. low
14. famous
15. studio
16. long
17. quickly
18. when
19. interesting
20. airplane
21. noisy
22. taxi
23. expensive
24. comfortable
25. expect
26. motorcycle

단어테스트 12

01. dangerous
02. lemon
03. sour
04. orange
05. important
06. friendship
07. brave

08. believe
09. be born
10. blood
11. thick
12. pen
13. mighty
14. sword
15. action
16. word
17. neighbor
18. distant
19. notebook
20. navy
21. white
22. pants
23. shirt
24. adult
25. high
26. mark

단어테스트 13

01. wide
02. lucky
03. animal
04. class
05. thin
06. watermelon
07. hard
08. slowly
09. difficult
10. surprising
11. singer
12. get
13. score
14. test
15. camel
16. pig
17. parrot
18. meaningful
19. January
20. short
21. exciting
22. island
23. also
24. mountain
25. grill
26. black

단어테스트 14

01. pork
02. ride
03. boring
04. merry-go-round
05. special
06. popular
07. kingdom

08. vote
09. diligent
10. restaurant
11. city
12. steak
13. honesty
14. fearful
15. subject
16. order
17. dish
18. step
19. potential
20. voice
21. trait
22. choice
23. world
24. song
25. kind
26. noisy

정답은 뒷면에서 확인하세요.

Circle and write.

알맞은 단어에 동그라미 하고 쓰세요.

1.

pose
pope

pope

2.
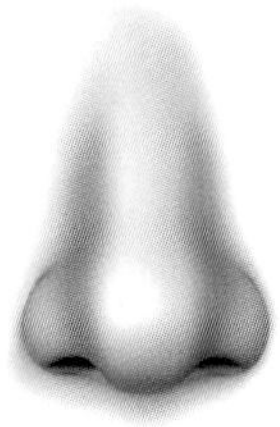

nose
nope

3.

rope
rose

4.

hope
hose

5.

note
nose

6.

slope
close

Circle and write.

알맞은 단어에 동그라미 하고 쓰세요.

1.

pose

pope

pope

2.

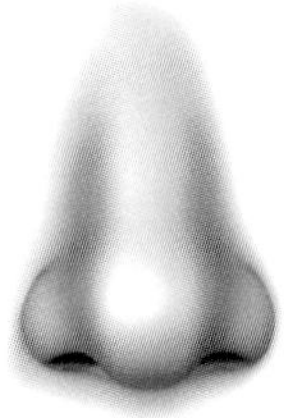

nose

nope

nose

3.

rope

rose

rose

4.

hope

hose

hope

5.

note

nose

note

6.

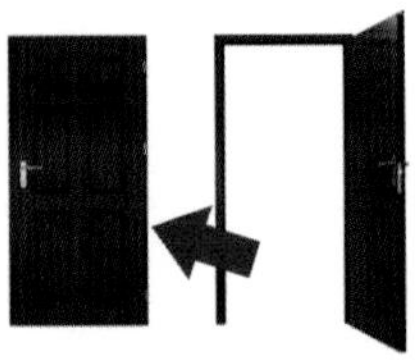

slope

close

close

MOTHERTONGUE
마더텅출판사
since1999.4.1.

초등영문법 3800제

정답과 해설

LEVEL 5

기본 1단계 부가의문문/수량형용사/There is · are 구문/비교급 · 최상급

초등영문법 3800제

정답과 해설

5

LEVEL

기본1단계

Chapter 01 부가의문문

Unit 01 부가의문문 (1)

Check and Write
▶ 본문 p.9

A 2. wasn't it? 3. are you?
B 2. is it 3. they

Unit 02 부가의문문 (2)

Check and Write
▶ 본문 p.11

2. didn't you
   You got a haircut, didn't you
   너는 머리를 잘랐어, 그렇지 않니?
3. can't he
   He can play soccer, can't he
   그는 축구를 할 수 있어, 그렇지 않니?
4. won't they
   They will help you, won't they
   그들은 당신을 도와줄 거예요, 그렇지 않나요?
5. aren't you
   You are from China, aren't you
   너는 중국에서 왔어, 그렇지 않니?
6. isn't she
   The baby is cute, isn't she
   그 아기는 귀여워, 그렇지 않니?

Practice 1
▶ 본문 p.12

A 2. isn't 3. aren't 4. wasn't 5. aren't
B 1. doesn't 2. didn't 3. don't 4. didn't 5. isn't
C 1. can't 2. won't 3. will 4. won't 5. can't
D 1. wasn't 2. did 3. did 4. didn't 5. didn't

Practice 2
▶ 본문 p.14

2. won't 3. went 4. looks
5. does 6. broke up 7. didn't meet
8. it 9. can 10. can't
11. doesn't 12. is 13. doesn't
14. she 15. doesn't 16. he
17. they 18. he 19. she
20. you

Practice 3
▶ 본문 p.17

2. can't he 3. does she 4. wasn't he
5. don't they 6. didn't she 7. don't they
8. doesn't she 9. can she 10. is it
11. doesn't it 12. didn't he 13. wasn't he
14. isn't it 15. wasn't it 16. don't they
17. are we 18. isn't it 19. will you
20. do you

Let's Practice More!

SET 01
▶ 본문 p.20

02. X 03. O 04. O 05. X
06. X 07. O 08. X 09. X
10. X 11. O 12. O

SET 02
▶ 본문 p.21

02. he 03. isn't 04. is 05. it
06. aren't 07. isn't 08. wasn't 09. it
10. wasn't 11. they 12. he
13. wasn't 14. were

SET 03
▶ 본문 p.22

02. isn't 03. can 04. doesn't
05. doesn't 06. isn't 07. don't 08. don't
09. do 10. isn't 11. aren't
12. doesn't 13. wasn't 14. does

SET 04
▶ 본문 p.23

02. did he 03. didn't she 04. doesn't he
05. didn't he 06. did she 07. can't he
08. won't you 09. can't you 10. doesn't he
11. doesn't he 12. can she 13. do you
14. didn't he

SET 05
▶ 본문 p.24

02. can 03. doesn't 04. isn't
05. don't 06. can 07. didn't
08. are 09. didn't 10. won't
11. won't 12. wasn't

SET 06
▶ 본문 p.25

02. did he 03. won't you 04. can't you
05. aren't we 06. wasn't he 07. didn't he
08. didn't they 09. doesn't she 10. isn't it
11. can't we 12. doesn't she 13. aren't they
14. did you

SET 07
▶ 본문 p.26

02. isn't it 03. can she 04. is he
05. doesn't he 06. doesn't she 07. can't you
08. can't he 09. don't you 10. will she
11. doesn't he 12. won't you
13. doesn't she 14. is it 15. can't we
16. isn't he 17. isn't she 18. can they
19. aren't they 20. does she

SET 08
▶ 본문 p.28

02. didn't they 03. isn't she 04. don't they
05. doesn't she 06. wasn't he 07. can't you
08. won't you 09. can't she 10. aren't they
11. don't they 12. didn't she 13. won't they
14. isn't he 15. isn't it 16. didn't he
17. didn't she 18. isn't she 19. can she
20. did she

Chapter 02 수량형용사

Unit 01 many와 much

Check and Write
▶ 본문 p.33

A 2. many 3. much 4. much
5. many 6. much

B 2. clothes
I don't have many clothes
나는 옷을 많이 갖고 있지 않아.
3. much
We had much rain yesterday
어제는 많은 비가 내렸어.

Unit 02 a lot of와 lots of

Check and Write
▶ 본문 p.35

A 2. much, a lot of, lots of

B 2. a lot of
I want to drink a lot of juice
나는 주스를 많이 마시고 싶어.
3. lots of
We make lots of mistakes
우리는 실수를 많이 해.

Practice 1
▶ 본문 p.36

A 2. much 3. much 4. many
5. much

B 1. many 2. much 3. many
4. much 5. many

C 1. much 2. Many 3. much
4. many 5. much

D 1. Many 2. Many 3. many
4. much 5. Much

Practice 2
▶ 본문 p.38

2. much 3. a lot of 4. much
5. many 6. a lot of 7. a lot of
8. lots of 9. a lot of 10. lots of
11. much 12. a lot of 13. many
14. a lot of 15. many 16. a lot of
17. lots of 18. much 19. many
20. a lot of

Practice 3
▶ 본문 p.41

2. I have much homework
나는 숙제가 많아.
3. I don't have much time
4. I have a lot of stress
나 스트레스 많이 받아.
5. I didn't take much rest
나는 많은 휴식을 취하지 못했어.
6. Many people worry about their health
많은 사람들이 그들의 건강을 걱정해.
7. You should not put a lot of sugar
8. We shouldn't drink too much coffee
우리는 너무 많은 커피를 마셔서는 안 돼.
9. You should not eat much salt
너는 많은 소금을 먹어서는 안 돼.
10. She learns many languages
그녀는 많은 언어들을 배워.
11. Did you spend a lot of time
12. I asked many questions
13. We took a lot of photos
우리는 많은 사진들을 찍었어.
14. He drinks lots of Coke
그는 많은 콜라를 마셔.
15. Mother Teresa helped a lot of people
테레사 수녀는 많은 사람들을 도왔어.
16. She heard a lot of good news
그녀는 많은 좋은 소식들을 들었어.
17. Many hands make light work
많은 손들이 일을 가볍게 만든다. (백지장도 맞들면 낫다.)
18. Many drops make a shower
많은 빗방울들이 모여 소나기를 만든다. (티끌 모아 태산이다.)
19. Too many cooks spoil the broth
너무 많은 요리사들은 수프를 망친다. (사공이 많으면 배가 산으로 간다.)
20. The world has many lessons

Let's Practice More!

SET 01
▶ 본문 p.44

02. much 03. many 04. many 05. much
06. much 07. many 08. much 09. many
10. much 11. much 12. many

SET 02
▶ 본문 p.45

02. much 03. O 04. many 05. O
06. O 07. much 08. many 09. many
10. O 11. much 12. O 13. O
14. much

SET 03
▶ 본문 p.46

02. many oranges 03. many lessons
04. many languages 05. much rest
06. many flowers 07. much bread
08. much time 09. many people
10. many pets 11. many dishes
12. many questions 13. much juice
14. many hands

SET 04
▶ 본문 p.47

02. much, lots of 03. many, lots of
04. much, a lot of 05. many, a lot of
06. many, lots of 07. much, a lot of
08. many, lots of 09. many, lots of
10. much, a lot of 11. much, a lot of
12. much, a lot of

SET 05
▶ 본문 p.48

02. O 03. O 04. O 05. X

06. O 07. X 08. O 09. O
10. X 11. X 12. X 13. O
14. O

SET 06
▶ 본문 p.49

02. C 03. C 04. UC 05. C
06. UC 07. UC 08. C 09. C
10. UC 11. C 12. UC 13. C
14. C

SET 07
▶ 본문 p.50

02. X 03. X 04. O 05. O
06. O 07. O 08. X 09. O
10. O 11. O 12. O 13. O
14. X 15. X 16. O 17. X
18. O 19. X 20. X

SET 08
▶ 본문 p.52

02. much 03. a lot of 04. lots of
05. much 06. much 07. a lot of
08. lots of 09. lots of 10. a lot of
11. Many 12. lots of 13. A lot of
14. lots of 15. lots of 16. many
17. lots of 18. many 19. much
20. a lot of

Unit 03 a few와 a little

Check and Write
▶ 본문 p.55

A 2. a little 3. a few 4. a little
5. a few 6. a little

B 2. dishes
I ordered a few dishes
나는 몇 개의 요리를 주문했다.
3. money
I just have a little money
나는 단지 조금의 돈을 가지고 있다.

Unit 04 few와 little

Check and Write
▶ 본문 p.57

A 2. little 3. few 4. few
5. few 6. little

B 2. little
He drinks little water
그는 물을 거의 마시지 않아.
3. cake
My sister ate little cake
내 여동생은 케이크를 거의 먹지 않았다.

Practice 1
▶ 본문 p.58

A 2. a little 3. little 4. a little 5. A few
6. a little 7. little 8. a few

B 1. a few 2. a little 3. little 4. few
5. a few

C 1. a little 2. a little 3. a few 4. a little
5. little 6. few 7. a little

Practice 2
▶ 본문 p.60

2. liltle 3. a little 4. a little
5. a little 6. little 7. a few
8. few 9. a little 10. a little
11. little 12. little 13. few
14. little 15. a little 16. few
17. a few 18. a few 19. little
20. little

Practice 3
▶ 본문 p.63

2. She has a few candies
그녀는 사탕 몇 개가 있어.
3. I have a few bananas
나는 바나나 몇 개가 있어.
4. A little chocolate is not harmful
조금의 초콜릿은 해롭지 않아.
5. I put on a few kilos
나는 살이 몇 킬로그램 쪘어.
6. I lost a few kilos
나는 살이 몇 킬로그램 빠졌어.
7. I have a few friends
나는 몇 명의 친구가 있어.
8. She bought a little bread
그녀는 빵을 조금 샀어.
9. I read a few books
나는 책 몇 권을 읽었어.
10. He drinks little Coke
그는 콜라를 거의 마시지 않아.
11. They read few books
그들은 책을 거의 읽지 않아.
12. I did a little homework
나는 숙제를 조금 했어.
13. I speak a little Spanish
나는 스페인어를 조금 해요.
14. I eat few vegetables
나는 야채를 거의 먹지 않아.
15. Dad has little time
아빠는 시간이 거의 없어요.
16. I have few friends
나는 친구가 거의 없어.
17. A few students are
18. We spent little time together
우리는 함께 보낸 시간이 거의 없었어요.
19. A few close friends live here
몇 명의 절친한 친구들이 여기에 산다.
20. Let me give you a little advice
너에게 조언을 조금 할게.

Let's Practice More!

SET 01
▶ 본문 p.66

02. a little 03. a little 04. a few
05. a few 06. a little 07. a little
08. a little 09. a few 10. a little
11. a few 12. a little

SET 02
▶ 본문 p.67

02. a little 03. a few 04. a few

05. a little 06. a few 07. a little
08. a little 09. a few 10. a little
11. A few 12. a few 13. A little
14. A few

SET 03 ▶ 본문 p.68

02. little 03. few 04. little
05. little 06. little 07. few
08. few 09. few 10. little
11. little 12. little 13. little
14. little

SET 04 ▶ 본문 p.69

02. few 03. little 04. little 05. little
06. few 07. few 08. little 09. little
10. few 11. little 12. Few

SET 05 ▶ 본문 p.70

02. few 03. few 04. a few
05. a few 06. few 07. a few
08. few 09. Few 10. A few
11. a few 12. few 13. a few
14. few

SET 06 ▶ 본문 p.71

02. a little 03. little 04. a little
05. little 06. a little 07. little
08. A little 09. little 10. a little
11. a little 12. little 13. a little
14. little

SET 07 ▶ 본문 p.72

02. a few onions 03. a little bread
04. a few hobbies 05. little time
06. few cousins 07. a few hours
08. a little salt 09. a little homework
10. few friends 11. A few students
12. little meat 13. a few bananas
14. a little sugar 15. little water
16. a few kilos 17. few troubles
18. few vegetables 19. a little milk
20. few books

SET 08 ▶ 본문 p.74

02. a little water 03. few oranges
04. little homework 05. little money
06. a few candies 07. a little time
08. little chocolate 09. few clothes
10. a little Korean 11. a little Coke
12. a little coffee 13. a few books
14. few flowers 15. little exercise
16. A few friends 17. a few kilos
18. a little meat 19. few eggs
20. little work

Unit 05 some과 any

Check and Write ▶ 본문 p.77

A 2. some
Can I ask some questions
제가 질문을 좀 해도 될까요?
3. any
Do you have any questions
질문들이 좀 있으신가요?

B 2. any
I don't need any help
저는 조금의 도움도 필요 없어요.
3. Some
Some people think he is crazy
몇몇 사람들은 그가 미쳤다고 생각해요.

Unit 06 all과 every

Check and Write ▶ 본문 p.79

A 2. every 3. all 4. every
5. every 6. all
B 2. month 3. is 4. are

Practice 1 ▶ 본문 p.80

A 2. any 3. some 4. some
B 1. any 2. some 3. any 4. any
5. some
C 1. every 2. every 3. All 4. All
D 1. has 2. all 3. any 4. every
5. Some

Practice 2 ▶ 본문 p.82

2. Did they have any problem with the car
그들의 차에 문제가 좀 있었던 거야?
3. All school buses arrived late
4. Do they need any help
그들에게 도움이 좀 필요할까?
5. Did you get any information
너는 정보를 좀 얻었니?
6. Everything will be fine
모든 것이 잘 될 거야.
7. Do you need any money
너는 돈이 좀 필요하니?
8. He doesn't work every Saturday
그는 매주 토요일에 일하지 않아.
9. We should find some solutions
우리는 해결책을 좀 찾아야해.
10. Do you have any idea
너 의견 좀 있어?
11. Did you ask any questions
너는 질문들을 좀 했니?
12. Can you lend me some comic books
나에게 만화책 좀 빌려줄 수 있어요?
13. I don't have any storybooks
나는 이야기책이 하나도 없어.
14. All my dreams will come true
내 모든 꿈들이 이루어질 거야.
15. can I borrow some rice
16. All my children are starving
나의 모든 자식들이 굶고 있어요.
17. Every cloud has a silver lining
모든 구름은 은빛 테두리(구름 뒤 햇살)가 있다. (어려운 상황에도 희망은 있다.)

18. Time heals all wounds
시간은 모든 상처를 치유한다. (시간이 약이다.)
19. Don't put all your eggs in one basket
너의 모든 달걀들을 한 바구니 안에 넣지 마라. (한 가지 일에 모든 것을 걸지 마라.)
20. Every garden may have some weeds
모든 정원에는 어느 정도의 잡초가 있다. (모든 것에는 약점이 있다.)

Practice 3

▶ 본문 p.84

2. I read some webtoons
나는 웹툰 몇 개를 읽었어.
3. I read them every Sunday
나는 그것들을 매주 일요일에 읽었어.
4. All my friends love them, too
내 모든 친구들도 그것들을 좋아하더라!
5. Every child needs friends
모든 아이들은 친구들이 필요해.
6. All dogs are children's best friends
모든 개들은 아이들의 최고의 친구들이야.
7. But some children don't like any dogs
하지만 몇몇 아이들은 강아지들을 조금도 좋아하지 않아.
8. I don't have any pets
나는 애완동물을 하나도 가지고 있지 않아.
9. I want some pets
나는 몇 마리의 애완동물들을 원해.
10. All Koreans eat rice
모든 한국인들은 쌀을 먹어.
11. I don't eat any rice
나는 쌀을 조금도 먹지 않아.
12. Some vegetables taste good
몇몇 채소들은 맛있어.
13. No way! All vegetables taste bad
그럴 리가! 모든 채소들은 맛없어!
14. Do you have any questions
질문들이 좀 있나요?
15. I asked some questions
나는 질문 몇 개를 했어.
16. Every student passed the exam
모든 학생들이 시험을 통과했어.
17. Would you like some ice cream
너 아이스크림 좀 먹을래?
18. Can I have some Coke
저 콜라 좀 먹어도 돼요?
19. I read two books every week
나는 매주 두 권의 책을 읽었어.
20. Every mother loves her daughter
모든 엄마들은 그녀의 딸을 사랑해.

Let's Practice More!

SET 01

▶ 본문 p.86

02. some　03. any　04. some
05. any　06. Some　07. any
08. any　09. Any　10. any
11. some　12. any

SET 02

▶ 본문 p.87

02. any　03. some　04. some
05. any　06. some　07. any
08. some　09. some　10. Some
11. any　12. any　13. some
14. some

SET 03

▶ 본문 p.88

02. All her money　03. All my dreams
04. All the teachers　05. All her friends
06. All my paintings　07. all the time
08. All the dishes　09. All my children
10. All the babies　11. All my friends
12. All the people　13. all the time
14. all your eggs

SET 04

▶ 본문 p.89

02. every　03. All　04. Every
05. Every　06. All　07. Every
08. All　09. All　10. Every
11. every　12. All

SET 05

▶ 본문 p.90

02. every　03. All　04. every
05. All　06. every　07. All
08. Every　09. All　10. Every
11. Every　12. all　13. Every
14. All

SET 06

▶ 본문 p.91

02. are　03. has　04. taste
05. needs　06. love　07. eat
08. loves　09. passes　10. are
11. is　12. praises　13. dance
14. sleeps

SET 07

▶ 본문 p.92

02. some Coke　03. some books
04. any help　05. any rice
06. any pets　07. any pets
08. some rice　09. any storybooks
10. Some vegetables　11. some pets
12. any problem　13. any problems
14. some healthy food　15. Some students
16. any idea　17. some books
18. Some children　19. Any child
20. some cookies

SET 08

▶ 본문 p.94

02. O　03. child　04. buses
05. dreams　06. O　07. O
08. O　09. praise　10. loves
11. day　12. has　13. O
14. O　15. paintings　16. week
17. O　18. O　19. Saturday
20. has

Chapter 01~02 실전테스트 ▶ 본문 p.96

01. ④ 02. a lot of
03. many[a lot of] 04. few
05. little 06. ① 07. ②
08. She can't[cannot] speak Italian, can she?
그녀는 이탈리어를 말할 수 없지, 그렇지?
09. (1) many (2) a few 10. ③ 11. ①
12. ①
13. (1) does he? (2) didn't we? 14. isn't
15. some 16. isn't it
17. doesn't he 18. a little
19. a few 20. much 21. (C)
22. is 23. students, eat 24. ①
25. ④ 26. ① 27. ②
28. did you 29. ① 30. ②

CH 03

Chapter 03 There is / There are

Unit 01 There is / are

Check and Write ▶ 본문 p.103

2. is
There is much milk
많은 우유가 있어.
3. are
There are three mushrooms
버섯 세 개가 있어.
4. is
There is an empty cup
빈 컵이 하나 있어.
5. are
There are fresh strawberries
신선한 딸기들이 있어.
6. is
There is a head of broccoli
브로콜리 한 송이가 있어.

Unit 02 There is / are의 과거 · 부정 · 의문형

Check and Write ▶ 본문 p.105

A 2. was 3. was 4. is
5. are 6. is
B 2. Are there
Are there any problems
무슨 문제 있니?
3. was
There was a small fight yesterday
어제 작은 다툼이 있었어.

Practice 1 ▶ 본문 p.106

A 2. is 3. are 4. Are
5. isn't 6. Are 7. is
8. Are 9. is 10. Were
B 1. is 2. There 3. is
4. Is 5. isn't 6. Is
7. there, is 8. Are
9. there, aren't 10. is

Practice 2 ▶ 본문 p.108

2. There are two children
두 명의 어린이들이 있어.
3. There are many friends
4. Are there dogs
5. there are
6. There are three dogs
7. Are there cats
8. there are not
9. There is delicious food
10. There was not a child
11. There were many students
12. There are a lot of things
13. There is not a student
14. There is juice
15. There were not any books
16. Is there a pencil case
17. There were many problems
많은 문제들이 있었어.
18. There is light at the end of the tunnel
터널의 끝에 빛이 있어.
19. Is there any problem
무슨 문제라도 있어?
20. there is not

Practice 3 ▶ 본문 p.111

2. There is a cat
3. Are there any chopsticks
젓가락 있니?
4. There is not[isn't] a tree
5. There are many dragonflies
6. Are there dragonflies
7. Is there a mother cat
8. there is not[isn't]
9. There were not[weren't] many comic books
만화책이 많이 없었어.
10. There is a piece of cake
케이크 한 조각이 있어.
11. There was not[wasn't] any time for a nap
낮잠을 잘 시간이 없었어.
12. There is not[isn't] a shortcut
지름길은 하나도 없어.
13. There were not[weren't] any chopsticks

14. Are there many video games
비디오 게임이 많이 있니?

15. There was not[wasn't] a way
방법이 없었어.

16. There are four potatoes
감자 네 개가 있어.

17. There was not any wind

18. Is there a subway station

19. There is a chocolate bar
초코바 한 개가 있어.

20. There are many ways
방법은 많아.

Let's Practice More!

SET 01 ▶ 본문 p.114

02. O	03. X	04. X	05. O
06. X	07. O	08. O	09. X
10. O	11. O	12. X	

SET 02 ▶ 본문 p.115

02. is	03. Are	04. were	05. is
06. was	07. are	08. are	09. is
10. is	11. Is	12. are	13. Are
14. are			

SET 03 ▶ 본문 p.116

02. There are	03. There is	04. There were
05. There is	06. There is	07. There was
08. There are	09. There is	10. There are
11. There are	12. There was	13. There were
14. There is		

SET 04 ▶ 본문 p.117

02. is	03. Were	04. are	05. Is
06. was	07. Are	08. Is	09. are
10. is	11. is	12. Are	13. Are
14. were			

SET 05 ▶ 본문 p.118

02. 있다	03. 있었다	04. 있다	05. 있다
06. 있었다	07. 있다	08. 있다	09. 있다
10. 있었다	11. 있었다	12. 있다	

SET 06 ▶ 본문 p.119

02. is not	03. is not	04. was not
05. are not	06. is not	07. was not
08. are not	09. were not	10. is not
11. are not	12. is not	13. were not
14. is not		

SET 07 ▶ 본문 p.120

02. Was there a tree
나무 한 그루가 있었어?

03. Are there many video games
비디오 게임이 많아?

04. Is there a dog on the street
길 위에 개 한 마리가 있어?

05. Are there five carrots
당근 다섯 개가 있어?

06. Were there many novels
소설이 많았어?

07. Was there a way
방법이 하나 있었어?

08. Were there many problems
많은 문제들이 있었어?

09. Is there delicious food on the table
탁자 위에 맛있는 음식이 있어?

10. Is there a monkey in the tree
나무에 원숭이가 한 마리 있어?

11. Was there a strong wind
강한 바람이 있었어(불었어)?

12. Is there a chocolate bar
초코바 한 개가 있어?

13. Were there many giraffe(s) at the zoo
동물원에 많은 기린들이 있었어?

14. Is there a sofa in the living room
거실에는 소파가 한 개 있어?

15. Is there much Coke in the bottle
병에 콜라가 많아?

16. Are there two children
두 명의 어린이들이 있어?

17. Are there many friends around you
네 주위에는 많은 친구들이 있어?

18. Are there three dogs in the yard
마당에는 세 마리의 개가 있어?

19. Is there bread on the table
탁자 위에 빵이 있어?

20. Is there one big lion
큰 사자 한 마리가 있어?

SET 08 ▶ 본문 p.122

02. there are	03. there aren't
04. there aren't	05. there is
06. there isn't	07. there is
08. there are	09. there aren't
10. there isn't	11. there is
12. there are	13. there aren't
14. there wasn't	15. there is
16. there was	17. there isn't
18. there are	19. there weren't
20. there isn't	

Chapter 04 비교급 / 최상급

Unit 01 비교급 (1)

Check and Write
▶ 본문 p.127

A 2. later 3. healthier 4. cheaper 5. busier
B 2. faster than

Unit 02 비교급 (2)

Check and Write
▶ 본문 p.129

A 2. more happily 3. more
4. more beautiful 5. better
B 2. more quietly
He speaks more quietly than others
그는 다른 사람들보다 더 작게 말해.

Practice 1
▶ 본문 p.130

A 2. colder 3. warmer 4. lower
5. more beautiful
B 1. more famous 2. taller 3. better
4. earlier
C 1. younger 2. older 3. longer
4. faster 5. slower 6. sooner
D 1. more quickly 2. happier 3. more
4. more interesting
5. more exciting

Practice 2
▶ 본문 p.132

2. A bus is noisier than a taxi
버스는 택시보다 시끄러워.
3. An airplane is more expensive than a taxi
비행기는 택시보다 더 비싸.
4. The train was more comfortable than
5. A motorcycle is more dangerous than a car
오토바이가 자동차보다 더 위험해.
6. Fruits are sweeter than vegetables
과일은 채소보다 더 달아.
7. A watermelon is heavier than a melon
수박은 메론보다 더 무거워.
8. Lemons are sourer than oranges
레몬은 오렌지보다 더 셔.
9. Vegetables are healthier than meat
10. Nothing is more important than friendship
우정보다 중요한 것은 없어.
11. You are braver than you believe
너는 네가 믿는 것보다 더 용감해.
12. My mother gets up earlier than I do
엄마는 나보다 더 일찍 일어나셔.
13. My twin sister was born earlier than me
내 쌍둥이 언니는 나보다 일찍 태어났어.
14. She was taller than me
그녀가 나보다 키가 컸었어.
15. Is she prettier than me
그녀가 나보다 예뻐?
16. Blood is thicker than water
피는 물보다 진하다.
17. The pen is mightier than the sword
펜은 칼보다 강하다.
18. Actions speak louder than words
행동은 말보다 큰 소리를 낸다. (행동이 말보다 더 중요하다.)
19. Two heads are better than one
하나보다는 둘이 더 낫다. (백지장도 맞들면 낫다.)
20. A good neighbor is better than a distant cousin
좋은 이웃이 먼 친척보다 낫다.

Practice 3
▶ 본문 p.134

2. cheaper 3. prettier
4. smaller 5. fatter
6. more interesting 7. more difficult
8. harder 9. higher
10. better 11. more quickly
12. smaller 13. more slowly
14. later 15. earlier
16. more tired 17. stronger
18. older 19. more
20. dirtier

Let's Practice More!

SET 01
▶ 본문 p.136

02. smarter 03. larger 04. colder
05. stronger 06. later 07. faster
08. longer 09. harder 10. cheaper
11. kinder 12. older

SET 02
▶ 본문 p.137

02. noisier 03. fatter 04. heavier
05. healthier 06. bigger 07. funnier
08. prettier 09. mightier 10. sadder
11. hotter 12. lazier 13. happier
14. earlier

SET 03
▶ 본문 p.138

02. more exciting 03. more easily
04. more slowly 05. more dangerous
06. more important 07. more quickly
08. more beautiful 09. more famous
10. more expensive 11. more heavily
12. more tired 13. more happily
14. more difficult

SET 04
▶ 본문 p.139

02. less 03. sooner 04. more
05. warmer 06. worse 07. slower
08. better 09. drier 10. more
11. lower 12. younger

SET 05
▶ 본문 p.140

02. colder 03. taller

04. more expensive
05. noisier
06. longer
07. more comfortable
08. healthier
09. prettier
10. louder
11. better
12. thicker
13. cheaper
14. more

SET 06 ▶ 본문 p.141

02. older
03. more slowly
04. more
05. earlier
06. later
07. sooner
08. lower
09. younger
10. more quickly
11. more
12. more exciting
13. more dangerous
14. more important

SET 07 ▶ 본문 p.142

02. than me
03. O
04. prettier
05. fatter
06. O
07. than English
08. O
09. better
10. more quickly
11. O
12. O
13. O
14. sweeter
15. braver
16. O
17. O
18. better
19. O
20. stronger

SET 08 ▶ 본문 p.144

02. sweeter than
03. more beautiful than
04. more famous than
05. better than
06. earlier than
07. warmer than
08. older than
09. sooner than
10. happier than
11. faster than
12. more comfortable
13. older than
14. later than
15. more than
16. heavier than
17. mightier than
18. more slowly than
19. louder than
20. bigger than

Unit 03 최상급 (1)

Check and Write ▶ 본문 p.147

A 2. widest 3. happiest 4. youngest
5. luckiest
B 2. smartest

Unit 04 최상급 (2)

Check and Write ▶ 본문 p.149

A 2. most difficult 3. most surprising
4. fattest 5. worst
B 2. hottest 3. best

Practice 1 ▶ 본문 p.150

A 2. biggest 3. tallest
4. fattest 5. smartest
6. oldest
B 1. most meaningful 2. coldest
3. busiest 4. shortest
5. most exciting
C 1. most beautiful 2. biggest
3. highest 4. most delicious
D 1. fastest 2. longest
3. most boring 4. most exciting
5. most popular

Practice 2 ▶ 본문 p.152

2. You got the most votes
너는 가장 많은 표를 받았어.
3. I'm not the smartest student
4. I am the most diligent student
5. Today is the greatest day
6. It is the most popular restaurant
7. What is the most delicious food
8. The steak is the most expensive item
9. Mom is the most fearful person
10. English is the most difficult subject
영어는 가장 어려운 과목이야!
11. I will order the cheapest dish
12. The first step is always the hardest
첫 걸음은 항상 가장 어렵다.
13. You may have the greatest potential
14. What are the most important traits
15. Charlie was the luckiest boy
16. She has the most beautiful voice
그녀는 가장 아름다운 목소리를 가지고 있어.
17. It was the worst choice
18. She is the shortest of them
그녀는 그들 중 키가 제일 작아.
19. Mount Everest is the highest mountain
20. Honesty is the best policy
정직이 최선의 방책이다.

Practice 3 ▶ 본문 p.155

2. She is the smartest girl
3. It is the most famous song
4. He is the kindest boy
5. He is the noisiest kid
6. The prettiest girl
7. My grandfather is the oldest
8. the most expensive chocolate
9. the youngest
10. the most interesting play
11. the most handsome actor
12. the worst movie
13. the most beautiful figure skater
14. the highest score
15. the fastest train
16. the happiest moment
17. the nicest sister
18. This is the cheapest t-shirt
19. They always do their best
그들은 항상 최선을 다해.
20. the best

Let's Practice More!

SET 01 ▶ 본문 p.158

02. the hardest
03. the cheapest
04. the longest
05. the highest

06. the tallest
07. the shortest
08. the greatest
09. the strongest
10. the smartest
11. the youngest
12. the coldest

SET 02 ▶ 본문 p.159

02. the easiest
03. the biggest
04. the hottest
05. the fattest
06. the saddest
07. the prettiest
08. the luckiest
09. the happiest
10. the heaviest
11. the busiest
12. the noisiest
13. the laziest
14. the dirtiest

SET 03 ▶ 본문 p.160

02. the most important
03. the most popular
04. the most boring
05. the most delicious
06. the most diligent
07. the most difficult
08. the most exciting
09. the most fearful
10. the most meaningful
11. the most expensive
12. the most interesting
13. the most beautiful
14. the most handsome

SET 04 ▶ 본문 p.161

02. the worst
03. the most slowly
04. the widest
05. the best
06. the nicest
07. the most
08. the latest
09. the most
10. the most famous
11. the least
12. the most surprising

SET 05 ▶ 본문 p.162

02. best
03. busiest
04. most popular
05. biggest
06. most boring
07. luckiest
08. worst
09. prettiest
10. nicest
11. youngest
12. happiest
13. most expensive
14. worst

SET 06 ▶ 본문 p.163

02. the biggest
03. the smartest
04. the oldest
05. the most delicious
06. the fastest
07. the most meaningful
08. the smartest
09. the hardest
10. the most important
11. the worst
12. the highest
13. the best
14. the most fearful

SET 07 ▶ 본문 p.164

02. tallest
03. most interesting
04. highest
05. oldest
06. fattest
07. most beautiful
08. shortest
09. cheapest
10. kindest
11. most exciting
12. smartest
13. noisiest
14. most delicious
15. most beautiful
16. fastest
17. highest
18. shortest
19. coldest
20. most

SET 08 ▶ 본문 p.166

02. the tallest
03. the most beautiful
04. more difficult
05. more expensive
06. older
07. the best
08. luckier
09. more interesting
10. fatter
11. the most difficult
12. the greatest
13. better
14. younger
15. the happiest
16. the best
17. the most diligent
18. taller
19. the greatest
20. heavier

Chapter 03~04 실전테스트 ▶ 본문 p.168

01. ①
02. ④
03. ②
04. more, than
05. fastest
06. ②
07. taller, than
08. most
09. the
10. ④
11. ②
12. was
13. are
14. were
15. ②
16. He is the funniest in our class.
그는 우리 반에서 가장 웃기다.
17. She is more beautiful than you.
그녀는 너보다 더 아름답다.
18. I am the fastest runner in our class.
나는 우리 반에서 가장 빠른 주자이다.
19. There are many students in the classroom.
교실 안에 많은 학생들이 있다.
20. There is a clock on the wall.
벽에 시계가 하나 있다.
21. Was Tom the best student in our class?
Tom이 우리 반에서 가장 뛰어난 학생이니?
22. Is there milk in the refrigerator?
냉장고 안에 우유가 있니?
23. English is more difficult than Korean.
영어는 한국어보다 어렵다.
24. Seoul is larger than Busan.
서울이 부산보다 크다.
25. Tom is taller than Jack.
Tom은 Jack보다 키가 크다.
26. English exam was easier than math exam.
영어 시험은 수학 시험보다 쉬웠다.
27. Tom is the smartest student.
Tom은 가장 똑똑한 학생이다.
28. This book is the most expensive in the world.
이 책은 세상에서 가장 비싸다.
29. Buddha is the wisest person in Indian history.
부처는 인도 역사에서 가장 현명한 사람이다.
30. He is the most famous singer in Korea.
그는 한국에서 가장 유명한 가수이다.

Game 정답

Game

아래 그림에 해당하는 단어를 찾아 동그라미 하세요.

R	S	M	B	A	N	A	N	A
W	T	P	Z	L	R	K	X	P
U	B	C	N	Q	U	C	S	P
G	J	H	A	D	M	J	A	L
A	L	E	O	R	A	N	G	E
L	F	E	X	T	R	I	N	Q
D	M	S	W	P	G	O	Z	C
K	I	E	P	O	T	A	T	O

초등영문법 3800제 서평

초등3학년 아이.. 원서는 어느 정도 잘 읽는데.. 글씨 쓰는 걸 많이 어려워해요. 그래서 문법을 알면 도움이 되지 않을까 싶어서 찾다가 3800제를 만났네요. 초등 저학년 아이가 혼자서 하는데 있어서 어려움이 없어요. 쉬운 단어로 설명을 해주니 쉽게 이해하고 공책에 배운 걸 써보기도 하면서 혼자서 열심히 공부하고 있어요. 2번, 3번 쭈욱~~ 3800제로 나갈까 합니다. **YES24** / 은**주

형이 중학교 진학 전부터 중학생용 3800제를 풀고 있었고 3800제 구성이 만족스러워서 초등 동생도 풀기 시작했어요. 개념도 구체적이고 다양한 내용이 있어서 좋았어요. 지루하지 않게 그림이 자주 삽입되어 있으니까 덜 삭막해요^^ 무엇보다 다각도로 연습문제가 진짜진짜 많아요. 어설프게 알고 진도 나가면 나중에 다시 봤을 때 까먹게 되고 제대로 이해 못하게 되거든요. 다양한 방식의 문제를 풀면서 영어실력이 확장되는 게 느껴져요. 게임, 마크만 성실, 꼼꼼하게 하지 공부는 대충 해치우고 마는 아이인데 이 교재를 통해서 언젠가는 영어 실력이 차곡차곡 쌓이길 기대해봅니다. 뒷편에는 단어 공부, 받아쓰기 연습을 할 수 있는 것도 있어요. 아이 핸드폰에 mp3파일을 넣어주면 스스로 할 수 있겠더라구요. 아직은 진도를 빨리 빼느라 숙제주진 않았는데 방학 시작하면 이 한권으로 영어공부는 충분할 것 같습니다. 핸드폰이 게임, 유튜브 보는 것만이 아닌 공부할 적에도 사용하는 것이라는 것을 알게 되길~^^; **YES24** / 희*

잠수네로 별칭되는 엄마표 영어를 한 지 몇 년 되었는데 엄마가 너무 띄엄띄엄 지도하다 보니 아이 단어와 문법이 많이 약한 것 같아 문법 교재로 구매했습니다. Unit 시작할 때 단어가 스물 몇 개 있고 의미를 인지하고 있는지 셀프 테스팅 하도록 구성되어 있고 개념 문제 뒤 연습문제가 쭉 있어서 아이가 스스로 정리하며 공부할 수 있어요. 난이도는 쉬운 편이라 차라리 부담 없이 스르륵 풀 수 있어서 좋아요. **YES24** / d**rh0424

문법은 실제로 문장 속에서 활용해봐야 이해가 쉽기 때문에 예제 중심의 반복학습이 가능한 책을 찾다가 선택한 교재입니다. 여러 형식으로 문제 풀이가 다양하게 제시되어 있어 문제를 풀다보면 그 원리가 절로 체득되어 정말 좋습니다. 아직 문법이라는 추상적인 개념을 이해하기 어려워하는 초등학생들에게 좋은 교재예요. 기존에 기초 문법의 틀이 조금 잡혀 있는 학생들은 자습용으로도 좋고 처음 문법을 접하는 학생들에게는 단계적으로 심화되는 문제 구성을 차근차근 밟아가며 공부하기에 좋습니다. **YES24** / a**owa

아이 문법 학습을 위해서 구입을 하게 되었습니다. 큰아이 중학영문법 3800제를 가지고 학습을 한 경험이 있어 믿고 구입하게 되었는데 역시나 초등문법도 많은 연습문제로 아이들이 같은 내용을 꾸준히 반복 연습하게 구성이 되어있어서 마음에 듭니다. 초등학생용이라 글씨도 큼직큼직하고 페이지마다 빈공간도 많이 있어 답답하지도 않아서 좋아요. 초등학생 아이들은 일단 글씨가 작고 빽빽하면 보면서 질려하는 경향이 있는데 이 교재는 그런 점에서는 후한 점수를 주고 싶네요. 단순 객관식 문제 풀이로 학습시키고 싶은 분들에게는 추천하지 않구요. 객관식 문제풀이가 단원 끝에 단원테스트에 조금 밖에 없어서요. 객관식 문제풀이가 아닌 아이가 문장을 만들면서 학습하기를 원하시는 분들에게는 강추합니다. 타 학습서들이 보통 초등문법을 2권 내지 3권에 끝내는 것을 이 초등영문법 3800제는 1권부터 8권까지에 연습할 부분을 나누어 놓았으니 얼마나 많은 반복을 시킬 수 있는지 권수만 봐도 알 수 있지요. 어쨌든, 초등학교 4학년 아이 8권까지 열심히 공부할 예정입니다. **YES24** / j**onim

book.toptutor.co.kr

구하기 어려운 교재는
마더텅 모바일(인터넷)을 이용하세요.
즉시 배송해 드립니다.

마더텅 학습 교재 이벤트에 참여해 주세요. 참여해 주신 모든 분께 선물을 드립니다.

이벤트 1 1분 간단 교재 사용 후기 이벤트

마더텅은 고객님의 소중한 의견을 반영하여 보다 좋은 책을 만들고자 합니다.
교재 구매 후, <교재 사용 후기 이벤트>에 **참여해 주신 모든 분**께는 감사의 마음을 담아 **모바일 문화상품권 1천 원권** 을 보내 드립니다. 지금 바로 QR 코드를 스캔해 소중한 의견을 보내 주세요!

이벤트 2 학습계획표 이벤트

STEP 1 책을 다 풀고 SNS 또는 수험생 커뮤니티에 작성한 학습계획표 사진을 업로드

필수 태그 #마더텅 #초등영어 #초등영문법3800 #학습계획표 #공스타그램
SNS/수험생 커뮤니티 페이스북, 인스타그램, 블로그, 네이버/다음 카페 등

STEP 2 왼쪽 QR 코드를 스캔하여 작성한 게시물의 URL 인증

참여해 주신 모든 분께는 감사의 마음을 담아 **CU 모바일 편의점 상품권 1천 원권** 및 **B 북포인트 2천 점** 을 드립니다.

이벤트 3 블로그/SNS 이벤트

STEP 1 자신의 블로그/SNS 중 하나에 마더텅 교재에 대한 사용 후기를 작성

필수 태그 #마더텅 #초등영어 #초등영문법3800 #교재리뷰 #공스타그램
필수 내용 마더텅 교재 장점, 교재 사진

STEP 2 왼쪽 QR 코드를 스캔하여 작성한 게시물의 URL 인증

참여해 주신 모든 분께는 감사의 마음을 담아 **CU 모바일 편의점 상품권 2천 원권** 및 **B 북포인트 3천 점** 을 드립니다.
매달 우수 후기자를 선정하여 **모바일 문화상품권 2만 원권** 과 **B 북포인트 1만 점** 을 드립니다.

B 북포인트란? 마더텅 인터넷 서점 **http://book.toptutor.co.kr**에서 교재 구매 시 현금처럼 사용할 수 있는 포인트입니다.

※자세한 사항은 해당 QR 코드를 스캔하거나 홈페이지 이벤트 공지글을 참고해 주세요.
※당사 사정에 따라 이벤트의 내용이나 상품이 변경될 수 있으며 변경 시 홈페이지에 공지합니다. ※만 14세 미만은 부모님께서 신청해 주셔야 합니다.
※상품은 이벤트 참여일로부터 2~3일(영업일 기준) 내에 발송됩니다. ※동일 교재로 세 가지 이벤트 모두 참여 가능합니다. (단, 같은 이벤트 중복 참여는 불가합니다.)
※이벤트 기간: 2024년 12월 31일까지 (*해당 이벤트는 당사 사정에 따라 조기 종료될 수 있습니다.)

정답은 뒷면에서 확인하세요.

Choose and write.

알맞은 것을 보기에서 골라 빈칸에 쓰세요.

보기 **ot** **ox** **op** **og**

1.

f [o] [x]

2.

d [ ] [ ]

3.

h [ ] [ ]

4.

d [ ] [ ]

5.

p [ ] [ ]

6.

b [ ] [ ]

Choose and write.

알맞은 것을 보기에서 골라 빈칸에 쓰세요.

보기 ot ox op og

1. 

fox

2. 

dot

3. 

hop

4. 

dog

5. 

pot

6. 

box